CONTENTS

PUBLISHERS
Plan-A-Home,
Lower Main Street,
Letterkenny, Co. Donegal.

Book Concept:
Harold McGuinness

ACKNOWLEDGEMENTS
Designs:
Harold McGuinness
Liam Cotter
Adam Leadley
Attracta Winters
Michael Hannigan
George McGuinness
Gavin Clinch
John Herlihy
Tom O'Donoghue

Editorials:
Cathy Doherty
Rosaleen McDaid
Louise Walsh

Quantity Surveying:
Harold McGuinness
Steven Barry

Computer Graphics
by InCADessence
Gavin Clinch
Paul McGrath
Shane McBrearty

Contributors
Attracta Winters   Interiors
Brendan Walsh   Gardens

Book origination/ make up:
InCADessence.
DBA Publications Ltd.,
56 Carysfort Ave, Blackrock,
Co. Dublin.

Printed by:
Universities Press,
Alanbrooke Road,
Belfast.

D0874915

Plan-A-Home

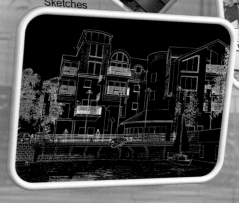

Introduction

Plan-A-Home's fifth issue 'Concepts for Irish Homes' has become the best produced and best selling book of house plans in the past decade. Our primary aim is to accurately inform all prospective home builders, consequently this edition contains further improved and enhanced designs as well as updated construction costs for all plans (current for the years 2003 and 2004) .

The house designs within this book are available directly from www.Plan-A-Home.ie via **On Line Plan Ordering Facility** or by simply contacting any of our offices throughout the country.

Plan-A-Home are unequalled as providers of plans and working drawings for prospective home builders and owners offering a comprehensive service we feel has yet to be surpassed.

In addition to houses from the book, HMG Associates and PAH Associates, our sister practices, offer a full architectural service covering all specialist design and construction procedures, from site surveys to design through planning applications and working drawings. HMG Associates and PAH Associates, offer a full supervision service managing the complete design and construction process from conception to completion.

Further information is included on pages 4,5 and 6 as to the services we provide, with an order form for all the houses offered in this book on page 159.

Whatever size of contract you are embarking on, we wish you well with your venture in the 21st Century.

Plan-A-Home

THE PLAN-A-HOME SERVICE:

FOR THE PROVISION OF UNALTERED PLANS

A simple and economical means of obtaining high quality plans and contract specification.
All plans are prepared to:

a high quality of design and presentation;

comply with current Building Regulations;

include your own specific choices of materials and finishes.

Please be sure that chosen plans suit your needs, if you are uncertain about anything you should obtain professional advice before ordering. For plans requiring alterations and for customised designs see next page.

TO ORDER YOUR PLANS

LoCALL **1850 222345** (local rate)
or 00 353 74 9129651 (outside Eire)
for the cost of your plans.

Plans range from €370 + vat

* **THEN** *

FILL out the forms on pages <u>159 & 160</u>

This service is ONLY available through PLAN-A-HOME.
Please allow up to 15 working days for delivery.

FOR ON LINE ORDERING PLEASE VISIT
www.plan-a-home.ie

ALL PLANS IN THIS BOOK ARE COPYRIGHT.
ONLY HMG ASSOCIATES AND PAH ASSOCIATES HAVE
THE FRANCHISE TO MAKE ALTERATIONS.

THE FULL ARCHITECTURAL SERVICE:
FOR CUSTOMISED DESIGNS

HMG Associates, Architects.   CMG Associates, Architects.

See inside back cover for office details and locations.

All of the following services are provided by HMG Associates throughout Ireland, and by CMG Associates in Cork. These architects retain the sole franchise from PLAN-A-HOME to work and alter any Plan-A-Home design to suit client needs.

Site Analysis and Survey

This is most important in ascertaining the house style to best suit your site and needs. Design style, proper aspect, best views, creating best impression at entrance to site, relationship to adjoining structures, planning constraints are some of the many concerns. Other information in relation to preparation of site maps for planning and tendering is observed and recorded on site.

Planning Permission

Preparations and submissions of all drawings, documents and notices required for planning applications. Liaison with the local planning authority should any difficulties arise during your application.

Working Drawings

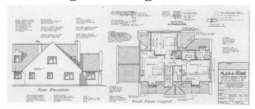

These are prepared after agreement has been reached on design sketches. Naturally some flexibility for change is still possible as final drawings near completion. Working drawings and specifications are to a standard that building contractors are fully aware of all details and finishes required, both for tendering and construction purposes, therefore eliminating unforeseen extras.

Design Consultation

Comprehensive discussions are required to determine your needs in order to prepare the initial sketch layouts. You may wish to bring the following to any design meeting:
a personalised wish list; this should include initial design brief ideas, special requirements, budget and any other relevant material.
From here we can, in simple steps, work towards an agreed final design.

Tendering Procedures

A list of builders to tender is normally drawn up by agrement between the Architect and client. Tender analysis i.e. thorough scrutiny of tenders, is fundamental to the successful awarding of any contract.

Quantity Surveying

Prior to finalising any design we strongly recommend that you avail of our Quantity Surveying Service. This runs in parallel with our Architectural service to establish construction costs and to highlight any design adjustments necessary to suit specific budgets. Having your scheme costs in advance is very useful when evaluating tender and budgeting for interim payments.

Supervision

Supervision of any project is highly recommended as the unsuspecting client can easily be caught out by contractual loopholes and the unscrupulous builder.

Supervision involves constant liaison with contractors, client and other members of the design team to achieve the best results and make certain that all efforts expended during design are strictly enforced. We ensure that all works and finishes are up to the highest standard and in compliance with Building Regulations, Planning and Mortgage Requirements.
In essence this service removes responsibility and liability for those who are in the process of building.

Structural Inspections

If full supervision is not required, structural inspections are advisable and indeed a prerequisite for most mortgage companies.
This involves:-
i) inspection of open foundation trenches.
ii) inspection of preparation of concrete ground floors.
iii) inspection of all roofing timbers and structures.
iv) inspection at practical completion.
* These services would be included within the full supervision package.

Site Inspection by HMG Associates

Commercial/Industrial

With professional teams of architectural staff both HMG Associates and PAH Associates handle all types of projects, from design to planning, tendering and supervision. This service is backed up with state of the art computerised drawing offices offering both flexibility in design and photo-realistic images.

Projects to date include:-

Projects to date include:

Commercial - Hotels
Shopping Units
Apartment Blocks
Filling Stations
Bars, Lounges, Restaurants
Tourism Projects
Nursing Homes
Industrial - Business Park
Fish Processing Plants
Storage & Retail Units
Fish Handling Units

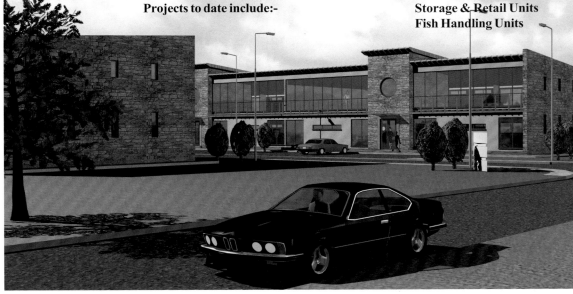

Housing Schemes

The Service includes:
Preliminary investigations, site suitability and analysis, full survey.
Design concepts for housing and site.
Working drawings, site layout, services drawings.
Bill of Quantities, relevant cost projections.
Tailored supervision requirements.
3-Dimensional computer modelling.

We offer a comprehensive service to potential developers.
Call into any of our offices to discuss your requirements. Office locations are given inside back cover.

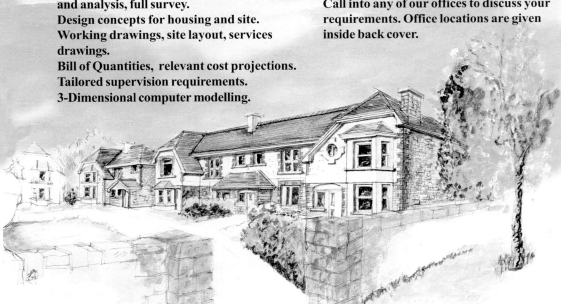

Initial Steps

The following is a list of important issues which you should ensure are in place before commencing construction on your new home:-

1. CHOOSING YOUR SITE

It is important to take into account that no two sites are alike and not all dwelling types are appropriate for every site.

It is necessary to make sure that your site can facilitate the many difficult aspects of the type of house you hope to build. (For further information see P118)

The nature of the soil and site gradients are of upmost importance when deciding on a site. Excessive filling or excessive excavation, can result in hefty expenditure.

Matters such as development cost, available services, and planning restrictions, are all contentious issues and therefore you should seek the help of your Architect. It is also possible to buy serviced sites from developers. This means that all drainage, water, electricity and other relevant services are provided onsite.

2. HOUSE PLANS:

There are an infinite number of possibilities and issues involved in designing a home. You will need one hundred percent effort on your behalf coupled with sound professional advice. The Architect is best qualified to give support in this area and to alleviate any anxieties you might have about design, acquiring planning, assisting with tender and construction supervision.

These services ensure that all the initial efforts and discussions which were planned and put on paper are instigated on site.

Time, effort and the assistance of a professional during the early stages and throughout the entire house building procedure can help avoid unwanted problems and ensure that you have a home that meets with your every expectation.

3. CONVEYANCING:

Ensure that the legal conveyancing of your site has been completed thoroughly in regard to site boundaries, easements for access or services, and any liability towards common accesses, or services clearly defined and highlighted. Have your site boundaries checked independently to ensure that they comply with your transfer documents.

4. MORTGAGING:

If you are arranging a mortgage this should be done before or in tandem with getting your house designs and permission so as to:-

(i) ensure that you can obtain sufficient funds to complete your home.

(ii) ensure that you comply with the many conditions laid down by your mortgage company in relation to structural checks, supervision, etc.

5. PLANNING PERMISSION:

Full planning permission must be received before any work can commence. Ensure also that any statutory objection periods which may exist, has elapsed, and any conditions outlined on your planning permission, are complied with during construction.

6. BUILDING REGULATIONS:

All plans and specifications should be to Building Regulation standards, and passed by the relevant authorities if applicable in your area. Likewise, you should ensure that contractor is fully conversant with the current Building Regulations, and fully intends to construct dwelling in compliance with same.

7. COMMENCEMENT NOTICE:

In the Republic of Ireland you are currently obliged to submit a Commencement Notice stating your intention to commence work within fourteen days. These forms can be obtained for your local authority.

8. INSURANCE:

Insurance cover is vital during course of construction to protect your investment. If under contract, then ensure that your builder has a policy to cover this, but if your building by the self-build method then insurance cover can be easily obtained through any broker.

9. STRUCTURAL INSPECTIONS:

a) **Home Bond Scheme.**

Builders registered under this scheme can offer you the additional security of a ten year structural guarantee against any major defects which may occur. Opting for a builder registered in this scheme, can often help to simplify mortgage applications, as it is a desired requirement with a lot of loaning agencies. The scheme is administered by the National House Building Guarantee Company, and inspections are carried out at three different stage during the course of construction, i.e. foundation trenches, roof and completion.

b) Supervision by architect/engineer: This is an alternative option if your builder is not registered in the above scheme or if you are going to self-build route, you should ensure that the persons employed to carry out the inspection are covered by professional indemnity insurance, although this may be a standard requirement of your mortgage.

Copyright

An Unauthorised Third Party architect will only give you a Second rate Service and leave you requiring a First Class Lawyer.

Use of Designs and Copyright Infringement
The Designs contained in this publication are the sole property of Plan-A-Home. It is illegal to use these designs in any form, either as illustrated or altered without the prior consent of Plan-A-Home.

Options for Obtaining Designs

Option 1
Standard Plans
All illustrated designs can be ordered directly through Plan-A-Home. Please refer to page 4 and the Order Form on pages 159 & 160

Option 2
Custom Design

The general concept of any of the illustrated designs can be altered and re-worked to suit your personal requirements. This service is provided through any of the HMG or CMG offices throughout the country, (see inside back cover). This service can also be provided together with a full architectural package as outlined on pages 5, 6 & 7

Please ensure that you adhere to one of the three criteria outlined above when using any of the illustrated designs in any form. Failure to comply with this has left us with no alternative but to prosecute those in breach of our copyright. Remember – Houses cannot hide!

You saw it here first – So if you like our ideas, lets do business.

Planning Interiors

The intention of this book is not to offer a finished solution to the potential house builder, rather it is a collection of proven ideas that may help generate a concept for your new home and aid you in discussion with us, the Architects. This Interior Design Section has been compiled in order to help you consider some of the factors having a bearing on the rooms within your home and to aid you in compiling ideas for your home.

External aspect and view have a direct bearing on how you inhabit your home and the plan layout of any building is as much generated by what is outside as what is needed inside. It is usual to take advantage of south westerly aspect for rooms which you inhabit in the evening and likewise some people wish to wake to morning sun and locate their bedrooms on the east facing side of their homes. The siting or facing direction of a new dwelling can be dictated by views or the location of adjacent dwellings. The need for connections or relationships between spaces or rooms can have just as much impact on the form a house takes.

We at Plan - A - Home are aware that the needs of no two people or families are the same and this is something we discuss at length with our clients when they first come to us. The more you can tell us about yourself the easier it is for us to create a home that is both tailored to your needs and which is also spatially attractive. Some of the most practical and also the most interesting spaces grow out of information that in the first instance did not seem to have much bearing so it is well worth considering all of your needs and at least some of the possibilities. Sometimes the easiest way to formulate the requirements for your new dwelling is to take a 'walk through' your imagined home room by room and make a record or wish list of what you want or hope to achieve in each space.

Paris Ceramics

HALLWAYS AND PORCHES

One of the functions of a hall or porch is to create an area between inside and out to allow visitors to shed their coats and to prevent draughts from sweeping into the rest of the house as they enter. A Hallway or porch may also be important as it gives that first impression to those arriving. As an entrance to your home it must be accessible to all users or visitors including those in wheelchairs and mothers with prams. You may have a specific piece of furniture that you want to display in the hallway such as a coat stand, hall stand, clock or you may want to hang photographs or pictures on the walls. It is important to allow space for such a purpose in advance. It may be appropriate to have the architect design built in spaces to accommodate seating, perhaps an area for the telephone, an alcove for display shelving or storage for coats, shoes and umbrellas. You may also wish to consider which other rooms it would be desirable to enter into from the hall and whether or not you would wish to be able to see into other spaces from the hall through glazed screens or partitions. It is important to be aware of natural lighting in the hallway. Very often the hall serves as the main circulation space and in many two storey homes the stair leads off the entrance hall, it is wise therefore to maximise natural lighting in order to decrease dependency on artificial lighting and conserve energy. A greater level of light can only afford greater safety to the stairway and it is also much more welcoming to enter a well-lit space. You may want to work on achieving a specific look or feel with your architect. A possibility would be the creation of a double height space or balcony feature. The feeling of change in level between rooms can also become a feature of a room and in particular of a hallway. It is also important to remember that the hallway is a 'public' space and it may be important to define the way for visitors into living rooms and away from for example a bedroom area.

LIVING ROOMS and LOUNGES

There are many titles for the room or rooms which are essentially gathering spaces in the home; living room, lounge, drawing room, family room, sitting room, parlour, den. These names probably have very different connotations for a lot of people but for the purpose of this section we will refer to the living room as the everyday room in regular use and which most likely is home to the television and the lounge as the more formal sitting room and which is most often where guests to the house are entertained. The decision to have two rooms rather than the one may be governed by the amount of entertaining you intend to do or by family members. It may be desirable for older children or teenagers to have their own sitting room.

Of course it is not necessary for every home to have two such rooms but where one does it is important to define their use and purpose and to make a stylistic difference between them. When planning your home we, the architects will guide you in giving preference to view and light when locating these rooms. It may be necessary to give them a similar aspect as the chances are they will be used at similar times of the day. In a contemporary home there are no hard and fast rules to which level in your home you locate rooms. A living room or lounge could quite easily be located on the first floor of a house. The living room as an everyday space could be formed as a mezzanine level with stair coming up from the kitchen. It may not be necessary to have a very large formal lounge and it could become a glazed reception or conservatory space off the entrance hall. It is possibly more important to be aware of the relationship you wish to have between a living space and other room types than in any other combinations. You may wish to have a formal lounge and only have a living room that is an annex of the kitchen / dining area. The connection between these spaces can often serve as a point of interest. Many people wish to build a wall or arch type division between these rooms. This can form an opening or the support for a glazed screen or doorway with views from one room into the other. A simple change in floor surface or level may be enough to define the space or a built in element such as a double sided fireplace can prove to be a more dramatic way of dividing the space. A practical element such as a fireplace has the purpose of being both a point of focus and also an ornament in a room can be important in giving character to that room.

You may also wish to consider using very different furniture arrangements to give an even greater contrast between a living room and lounge. This choice may be relevant in defining the shape of the rooms.

KITCHENS.

There are really several possibilities in terms of types of kitchen depending on how you see the room functioning. It may be more practical for you to have a Utility Room entirely independent of the Kitchen. The following are varying ways of defining the kitchen area and may or may not require separate Dining and Utility Areas.
The Kitchen for Cooking, the Kitchen / Living and the Kitchen / Dinette

The Kitchen for Cooking

Some people prefer to have a kitchen solely designated for the preparation of food and entirely separate from the dining room. In this case possibly more than in other types of kitchen the relationship between the sink, cooking appliances and work surface is paramount. The height and location of appliances and units may also be dictated by the needs of the user. Wheelchair users prefer to have units at a lower level often with pullout work surfaces so that they can comfortably work from their chair. Those with back or hip problems find slightly higher units more accommodating. The enthusiastic chef may have particular requirements in terms of working surfaces and appliances. Separate sinks for food preparation and dish washing may be necessary. Accessible storage places for implements such as food processors and ingredients may also be important.

One of the most important things to be able to control in a kitchen is the environment. Lighting and ventilation both natural and artificial are also of great importance in the kitchen in order to maintain a comfortable working environment This also means that switches, controls, means of escape and safety measures must accommodate all users. These points are relevant to all kitchens and not solely this type of kitchen.

Alternatively you may regard cooking and the kitchen as undesirable and therefore wish to keep the size of the kitchen to a minimum. However it is important to strike a balance and avoid having a room which is poky or unpleasant to be in. Glazing for light and view can be just as important in a functional room as it is in a recreational one.

The Kitchen / Living

The kitchen is increasingly superseding the living room as the most important room by becoming the heart of the home and the centre for gathering, cooking and dining. In many ways this type of kitchen is associated with the look, feel and function of the farmhouse kitchen. Such a room has many requirements and therefore several spaces may need to be defined within the room. The Range and Aga are increasingly growing in popularity. A large functional item such as a Range needs to be located with a degree of care as it acts as both a heat source and also the focal point of the room. It is most important that if you wish to have a range in your new home that you discuss this in advance with the architect as certain measures need to be taken.

Circulation is important around the sink and hob areas and is also an important issue if you intend to have an island work unit. Island units are becoming increasingly popular but they must be planned meticulously if they are to function properly and not become cumbersome to the working of the kitchen. Discussion with the architect is the best way to assess if an island unit is practical in your kitchen in relation to its size and other fittings that may be more necessary. On the plus side an island unit can be most beneficial from the point of view that those working at the unit can interact socially with others in the room instead of in the case of traditional units where the worker often has his or her back to others in the room. You may wish to consider that in a multi-functional kitchen a fitted kitchen is not always the most practical solution. A combination of a built-in larder, some fitted cupboards and perhaps a free standing piece of furniture such as a dresser or shelves can be more flexible and in the long run can

be renewed and updatedoften at less cost than a complete fitted kitchen. Most importantly if you do wish to have a multi-functional kitchen living space do plan for it in advance. If you want to include space for a sofa and armchairs or television or a play area for children allow for it in advance and avoid having a space that is uncomfortable or unworkable.

Kitchen / Dinette

This combination is often used in conjunction with a formal dining room or as an alternative to. If you intend to have a dining room and use it on a regular basis then the dinette area of the kitchen can be kept to a minimum perhaps restricted to a breakfast bar type arrangement or taking the form of a built in diner type booth. This can become a useful space for children to do homework or perhaps even to take the idea farther the space could be curtained or partitioned with seating forming a caravan bed arrangement and doubling as a spare room annex. If the Dinette is to be the main space for eating at meal times it is important to define the dinette from the kitchen area. Some of the devices for splitting or making contrast between spaces mentioned in the Living Room Section can also be applied here such as change in surface finish or level. Kitchen units can also be arranged to create a division between the two areas.

DINING ROOM

Some people wish to have a formal dining room albeit for every day or special occasion usage. Generally it makes sense to have the dining room as close to the kitchen as possible and often it is favourable to have a connecting door or hatch between the two rooms so that food can be moved from one to the other with ease. If the Dining Room is to be used for entertaining guests it may also be

Neville Johnson

preferable to have it adjacent to the lounge. Generally rooms for entertaining guests have a south westerly aspect to avail of evening light when most entertaining occurs. A view of the garden or even doors onto an external patio area could be appropriate perhaps to facilitate barbecues on summer evenings. Internally the size of space will be important depending on how many people you wish to be able to accommodate at any one time and also in terms of what furniture you intend to use within the room. It will be important to be able to control the heating, ventilation and lighting of the dining room in order to create a pleasant atmosphere and to ensure the comfort of your guests.

UTILITY ROOM

In the larger family home it is often preferable to have a laundry or utility room entirely separate from the kitchen. In a functional space such as the utility room people are very often more aware of their requirements in advance. The utility room is most likely to be the location for a washing machine and tumble dryer but could also provide space or a

Laura Ashley

location for any of the following: a boiler, a fridge freezer, clothes drying area, hotpress, mending and ironing space with either permanent or collapsible ironing board, a sink for washing or vegetable preparation or both, a WC, area for pets and storage, either built in shelves or presses or wall mounted units. Careful consideration should be given to exactly what items are to be stored in the Utility Room as often kitchen type units are inappropriate. Quite simply the Utility room could be the smallest room in the house but it could also have the greatest demand put on it in terms of what is needed and therefore the greatest care is required in assessing exactly what the usage of the utility room will be and planning for it in advance. If your needs are currently

Neff/Kal

quite modest but likely to change in the future for example if your family size were to increase, this is one area where it would be wise to allow for the change in advance. The Utility may also serve as a back porch to the kitchen and therefore conserving heat to the kitchen or you may prefer to be able to have a separate back porch if the back door is to be used in preference to the front entrance and allow the utility to function solely as a working space. It is often appropriate particularly in rural dwellings to allow a porch area with easily cleaned floor surface and space for coats and muddy shoes.

BATHROOMS

The planning of a Bathroom can also be dependant on its proximity to other rooms and on what other washing facilities are provided elsewhere in the home. If you have en-suite shower rooms to each bedroom in the house you may question the need for a bathroom at all or it may need only to be very small. However for many the luxury of a bath is too much to forgo. Increasingly the bathroom is treated not merely as functional but as a place of relaxation and leisure with many bathrooms incorporating saunas and Jacuzzi features. If the bathroom is to incorporate a leisure feature and be used by more than one person at a time the fittings may need to reflect this, for example a double shower may be appropriate. This may also be a consideration if the family have young children. The bathroom layout is extremely important as once the sanitary fittings are positioned they are unlike other furniture in that they can not be easily moved. It is worth considering the alternatives to the traditional bathroom layout with bath along one wall and basin and toilet on the other. The mobility of family members whether it be an older person or a wheelchair user can have a bearing on the type and location of fittings. There are many possibilities for interesting and practical bath and shower room layouts. A long narrow bathroom could

Aqua Maison

allow basin, shower and bath to be built into one wall in an arrangement that incorporates shelving space for towels and bathing products and recessed lighting for effect. A bath can take on added grandeur if either raised above or sunk into the floor. Once again it will be necessary to consult your architect on whether or not a feature such as this may be feasible within the structure of your new home.

BEDROOMS

All bedrooms have different requirements in terms of who the user is and what their preferences are. Again there are no hard and fast rules for where bedrooms are located within the home. Some people wish to sleep at the top of their homes with a view of the night sky from their beds and others like the notion of being able to open French doors onto a garden space. For many, more practical requirements govern their sleeping arrangements; the need to be near a bathroom or children's rooms at night.

THE MASTER BEDROOM

The Master Bedroom is often regarded as a haven away from the clutter of the rest of the house. Often this minimalism is achieved by the creation of a large walk-in wardrobe or dressing room off the master bedroom. In planning terms a walk-in wardrobe is not really an excessive use of space if you consider that it takes up an area comparative to two large built in wardrobes. The walk-in wardrobe can become an invaluable storage space if the interior is given careful consideration. The entire area of the room from floor to ceiling can be utilised for racks, shelving and drawers. The inclusion of a storage space such as this also can be an advantage in that less furniture is needed in the bedroom and the room can become much smaller and hence easier to heat. Most of the plan layouts in this edition indicate both built in storage space and also space for occasional furniture. Wall space can be important in terms of free area for locating furniture if two or more walls contain glazing or doorways.

There has also been a growing trend towards the inclusion of an en-suite bath or shower room off the Master Bedroom. The en-suite is governed by the same issues as discussed with regard to bathrooms although may have greater constraints in terms of area, plumbing and ventilation again all of which the architect will be able to give you guidance on.

CHILDREN'S BEDROOMS AND PLAYROOMS

A child's room may have to alter radically in order to facilitate the changing needs of that child as they mature. What is certain is that from babyhood right through to teenage years storage and work space of some sort will be required unless this is to be facilitated by a purpose built play room or study. In a child's work or play area be it separate from or within the bedroom lighting is again an important issue. Safety either with regard to both windows and electrical fittings must also be adhered to. It may be more appropriate to have fitted wall lights serving as desk and bedside lights rather than to have a free standing lamp with a flex that could easily be tripped over. Items such as light fittings may increase the cost of your home in the short term but in the long run this is outweighed by the practical purpose they serve. Children's rooms should allow them personal space particularly if the room is to be shared. This personal space can be all the more exciting if seen to be different from what other friends have. Built in bunks or window seats can provide extra storage and free up floor space whilst also providing private nooks within the room. It is worth remembering that a room created as a playroom can be reinvented as a study, bedroom or living room as your family requirements change.

Scorpio Furniture Ltd.

STUDY AND WORK SPACES

In our society more and more people are finding it necessary to have an area to work or study in at home or alternatively they have a hobby or leisure past-time that has spatial requirements. This type of space generally needs to be a self-contained with good lighting and if possible a pleasant aspect or view. If you are to receive clients or colleagues the space will need to be distanced from domestic

Neville Johnson Furniture

activities and the private areas of your home. It may not be viable for you to give a room entirely over for use as work space so forming an annex off another room or creating a room which has dual purpose may be more satisfactory. The American 'den' type room with space for desk, files and books is coupled with comfortable seating and recreational facilities. A work space often needs space both to leave work out and to store it away. You may have other requirements for example in terms of electricity or water supply. Alternatively your work or hobby may require access to outside for example for carpentry you may need to bring in timber from an external store. Specialist rooms can also require particular types of finishes or space to facilitate equipment. The Architect can advise you on how all these requirements can be met.

SUN ROOMS AND CONSERVATORIES

The most important consideration when planning a Sun room or Conservatory is aspect. These rooms should face south or south west if they are to benefit from the light and heat of the sun. If you intend to have a room like this in your home either straight away or at a later date it, provision will need to be made now when prioritising the location of one room over another and also to ensure there is enough external area to make the addition viable.

The Sun Lounge or Conservatory should be integral to the design of your home. It is important to decide the type of usage that the room is to have and whether or not it will be appropriate to have the space as an annex to another room. A sun lounge could serve as a dining area accessed off the kitchen. Alternatively you may wish the space to function independently of other rooms and have its own separate entrance for example if it is to act as a living room. Whatever the usage, the room must be planned accordingly to allow for furniture. The same principles that we have discussed in relation to other room types apply; the connection between room and the relationship with internal and external spaces. A further consideration which may be governed by the

usage of the room is the type of roof to be used. Conservatories are traditionally a fully glazed space, however it has become increasingly popular to have a conventional roof-type over the conservatory often with a roof light as a combined feature of the structure. This type of roof allows for much less heat loss than a glazed roof and may be more appropriate for a room which is to be used all year round. A conventional roof can also be underdrawn with exposed timbers used to stylistic effect.

The relationship with external space is paramount where the Sun Lounge is to open up onto garden space. This arrangement will need to be considered not only as part of the internal planning but also as a continuation of the external landscaping. In theory the sun lounge will open up onto the sunniest part of the garden and this is therefore is the ideal location for a patio. Patio Design and Hard Landscaping is discussed in greater detail in the Landscape Section of this book. The Sun Lounge is an ideal environment to grow plants in as it performs similarly to a greenhouse. Plants form screening from the sun and also create a pleasant effect as light filters through the greenery. It is possible to build internal beds for planting within the space and to create a self watering facility to these.

Special consideration should be given to fabric and finishes within a Sun Lounge or Conservatory space as they are more likely to fade within this type of environment. Blinds and other sun screening devices may need to be employed.

Imperial - Metric Conversion

3'0"	0.92	16'0"	4.86
3'4"	1.02	16'4"	4.98
3'8"	1.12	16'8"	5.08
4'0"	1.22	17'0"	5.18
4'4"	1.42	17'6"	5.34
4'8"	1.53	18'0"	5.49
5'0"	1.63	18'6"	5.64
5'4"	1.73	19'0"	5.79
5'8"	1.83	19'6"	5.94
6'0"	1.94	20'0"	6.10
6'4"	2.03	21'0"	6.40
6'8"	2.13	22'0"	6.71
7'0"	2.24	23'0"	7.01
7'4"	2.34	24'0"	7.32
7'8"	2.44	25'0"	7.62
8'0"	2.54	26'0"	7.93
8'4"	2.64	27'0"	8.23
8'8"	2.74	28'0"	8.54
9'0"	2.85	29'0"	8.84
9'4"	2.95	30'0"	9.15
9'8"	3.05	31'0"	9.45
10'0"	3.15	32'0"	9.76
10'4"	3.25	33'0"	10.10
10'8"	3.35	34'0"	10.37
11'0"	3.45	35'0"	10.67
11'4"	3.56	36'0"	10.98
11'8"	3.66	37'0"	11.28
12'0"	3.76	38'0"	11.54
12'4"	3.86	39'0"	11.89
13'0"	3.96	40'0"	12.19
13'4"	4.06	45'0"	13.72
13'8"	4.16	50'0"	15.42
14'0"	4.27	55'0"	16.77
14'4"	4.37	60'0"	18.29
14'8"	4.47	65'0"	19.82
15'0"	4.57	70'0"	21.34
15'4"	4.62	75'0"	22.86
15'8"	4.77	80'0"	24.39

Stepped or Sloping Sites

We have included a number of designs with stepped floor levels appropriate to sloping sites. Although all designs may be adapted to suit such sites we would recommend that you take further consultation prior to a design choice. Designs shown with stepped floors can, of course, be adapted for flat sites.

Grant Sized Dwellings

These designs are all under 1346 sq. feet and are therefore eligible for a new house grant. We have striven to offer a full spectrum of design alternatives within this section. Most layouts have the flexibility to be increased or reduced to suit individual financial requirements.

Vernacular Elements

These designs are what we consider to contain elements of established Irish vernacular. They offer obvious appeal to people looking for traditional design.

Suitable for Conversion

These dwellings have been designed specifically for possible future expansion, either by increasing floor area or utilising the roof space. These designs may suit people with long term budget plans

Attached or Integral Garages

This symbol denotes where a garage may be added or is included. Although in some cases it may not form an integral part of the building it can be built at the same time, therefore offering financial savings whilst maintaining the buildings integrity.

A typically illustrated Floor Plan

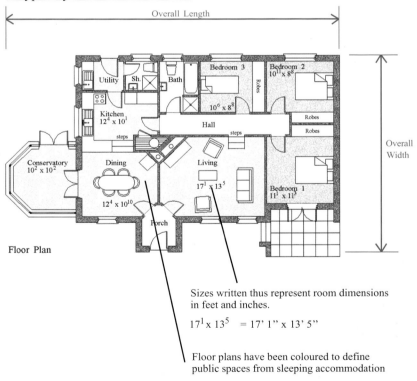

Floor Plan

Sizes written thus represent room dimensions in feet and inches.

$17^1 \times 13^5 = 17' 1'' \times 13' 5''$

Floor plans have been coloured to define public spaces from sleeping accommodation

Please Note:

Floor Areas given do not include garages (where these exist).

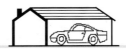

No.1

Overall Length 41'03"
Overall Width   21'08"
Garage   351 sq.ft.
Store   176 sq.ft.
Compound   77 sq.ft.

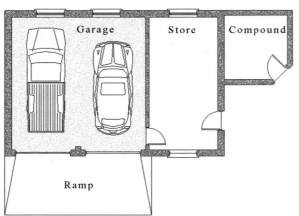

Garage   Store   Compound

Ramp

No.2

Overall Length 16'01"
Overall Width   28'03"
Floor Area   344 sq.ft.

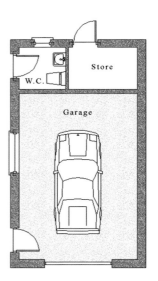

Store

W.C.

Garage

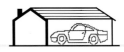

No. 3

Overall Length 21'10"
Overall Width 15'08"
Floor Area 267 sq.ft.

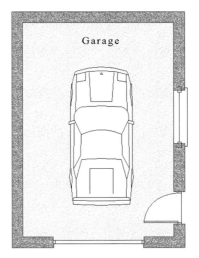

Garage

No. 4

Overall Length 26'00"
Overall Width 21'08"
Floor Area 473 sq.ft.

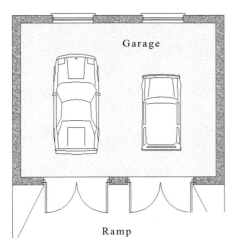

Garage

Ramp

Three Bedroom

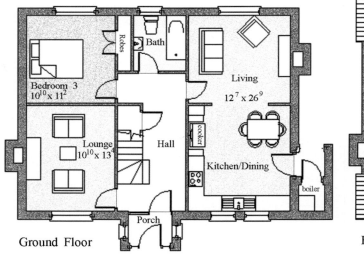

Ground Floor

Bedroom 3
10^{10} x 11^2

Robes

Bath

Living
12^7 x 26^9

Lounge
10^{10} x 13^4

Hall

cooker

Kitchen/Dining

boiler

Porch

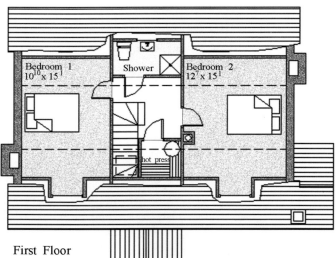

First Floor

Bedroom 1
10^{10} x 15^1

Shower

Bedroom 2
12^7 x 15^1

hot press

Overall Length	34'04"
Overall Width	26'09"
Ground Floor	829 sq.ft.
First Floor	515 sq.ft.
Floor Area	1344 sq.ft.

An open plan kitchen/dining and living space is a notable aspect of this plan. This design has scope for diversification from the layout shown here.

Plan-A-Home
Have offices in Donegal, Dublin, Cork and Galway. See inside back pages for addresses.

 £G

Additional Options and Services Available. See page 17.

Three Bedroom

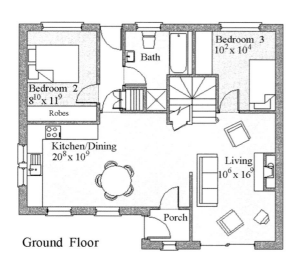

Bedroom 3
10^2 x 10^4

Bath

Bedroom 2
8^{10} x 11^9

Robes

Kitchen/Dining
20^8 x 10^9

Living
10^6 x 16^9

Porch

Ground Floor

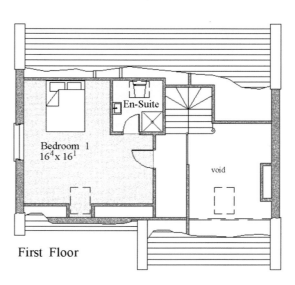

En-Suite

Bedroom 1
16^4 x 16^1

void

First Floor

<u>Construction Costs</u>
For a guideline of costs
in Section A see pages
48 and 49.

This enthusiastically received and versatile dormer
dwelling is contemporary reworking of traditional
elements. It has interesting open plan living spaces
with balcony overlooking the sitting room.

Overall Length	33'05"
Overall Width	24'11"
Ground Floor	771 sq.ft.
First Floor	323 sq.ft.
Floor Area	1094 sq.ft.

Additional Options and Services Available. See page 17.

Three Bedroom

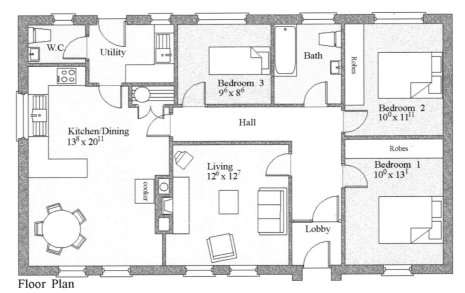

Floor Plan

Overall Length   44'03"
Overall Width   27'04"
Floor Area   1076 sq.ft.

A discreet cottage type dwelling with simple
detailing distinguishing the front doorway.
Internally there is a roomy kitchen/dining area.

<u>Construction Costs</u>
For a guideline of costs
in Section A see pages
48 and 49.

Additional Options and Services Available. See page 17.

Three Bedroom

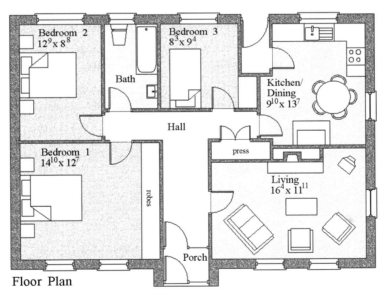

Bedroom 2
12^9 x 8^8

Bath

Bedroom 3
8^3 x 9^4

Kitchen/ Dining
9^{10} x 13^7

Hall

Bedroom 1
14^{10} x 12^7

robes

press

Living
16^4 x 11^{11}

Porch

Floor Plan

<u>Plan-A-Home</u>
For Construction Cost
Consultants and Quantity
Surveyors.

This dwelling makes strong reference to traditional
Irish design. It has scope for conversion; adding
bedrooms within the roof space and replacing
bedroom 3 with a staircase and small utility.

Overall Length 38'09"
Overall Width 27'09"
Floor Area 960 sq.ft.

Additional Options and Services Available. See page 17.

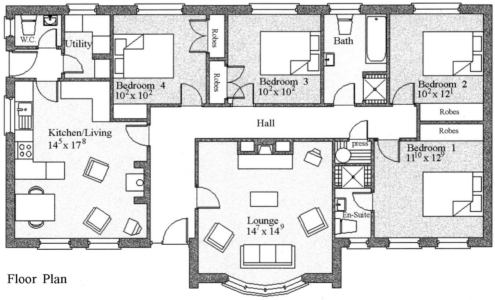

Floor Plan

Overall Length 53'00"
Overall Width   27'02"
Floor Area   1345 sq.ft.

The coupling of a hipped roof and bay window draws
attention to the living room at the heart of this house.
The kitchen/dining area is a compact space with a
range as a focal point.

Plan-A-Home
For interior planning
and design.

Additional Options and Services Available. See page 17.

Four Bedroom

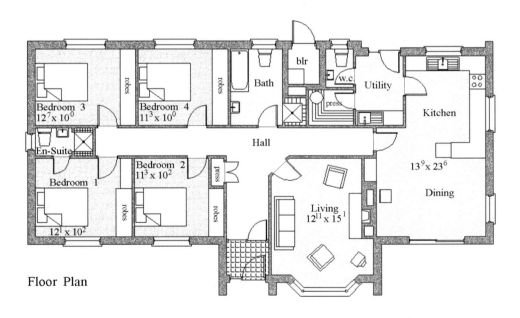

Floor Plan

Bedroom 3
12^7 x 10^0

Bedroom 4
11^3 x 10^0

En-Suite

Bedroom 1
12^1 x 10^2

Bedroom 2
11^3 x 10^2

robes

robes

press

robes

robes

Bath

blr

w.c

Utility

press

Hall

Kitchen

13^9 x 23^6

Dining

Living
12^{11} x 15^1

Construction Costs
For a guideline of costs
in Section A see pages
48 and 49.

The integration of porch and bay is a pleasing feature
of this simple bungalow. This type of hipped roof is
not indigenous to all areas and a traditional gable
may be more appropriate.

Overall Length 58'09"
Overall Width 26'05"
Floor Area 1474 sq.ft.

Additional Options and Services Available. See page 17.

Three Bedroom

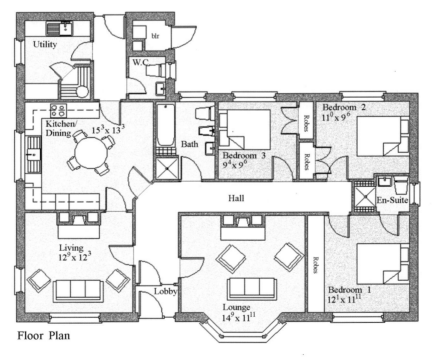

Floor Plan

Overall Length 47'09"
Overall Width 38'01"
Floor Area 1345 sq.ft.

A sound, modest bungalow with an understated facade, clean lines and a simple living room bay.

Construction Costs
For a guideline of costs in Section A see pages 48 and 49.

Additional Options and Services Available. See page 17.

Four Bedroom

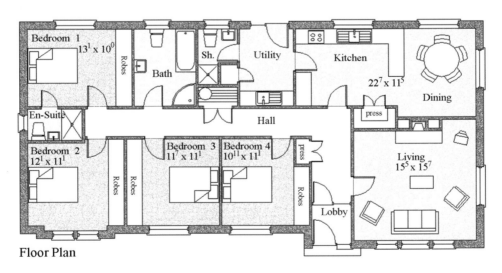

Floor Plan

Bedroom 1 13¹ x 10⁰
Robes
Bath
Sh.
Utility
Kitchen 22⁷ x 11⁵
Dining
press
Hall
En-Suite
Bedroom 2 12¹ x 11¹
Robes
Bedroom 3 11⁷ x 11¹
Bedroom 4 10¹¹ x 11¹
press
Robes
Living 15⁵ x 15⁷
Lobby

Plan-A-Home
For comprehensive
Specification Documents

A simple arrangement of the basic elements.
Painted fascias and barge boards are not
always appropriate and obviously require
maintenance.

Overall Length 58'04"
Overall Width 22'04"
Floor Area 1480 sq.ft.

For Metric/Imperial conversion table see page 17.

Three Bedroom

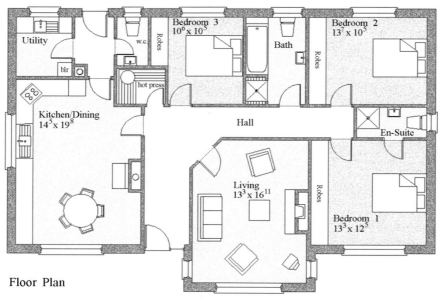

Floor Plan

Bedroom 3
10⁶ x 10⁵

Bedroom 2
13⁷ x 10⁵

Utility

w.c.

Robes

Bath

Robes

blr

hot press

Kitchen/Dining
14⁵ x 19⁸

Hall

En-Suite

Living
13³ x 16¹¹

Robes

Bedroom 1
13³ x 12⁵

Overall Length 49'02"
Overall Width   29'02"
Floor Area   1345 sq.ft.

A softer line house with elegant hipped roofscape.
This dwelling has spacious kitchen/dining areas
with a centrally located living room.

Plan-A-Home
For information on
house grants.

Additional Options and Services Available. See page 17.

Three Bedroom

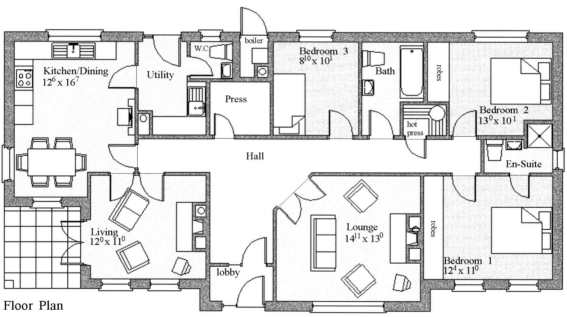

Floor Plan

Bedroom 3
8^{10} x 10^1

Bath

Bedroom 2
13^0 x 10^1

En-Suite

Kitchen/Dining
12^6 x 16^7

Utility

W.C

boiler

Press

robes

hot press

Hall

Living
12^0 x 11^0

lobby

Lounge
14^{11} x 13^0

robes

Bedroom 1
12^4 x 11^0

<u>Construction Costs</u>
For a guideline of costs
in Section A see pages
48 and 49.

A South/ South West aspect would be beneficial to
the living areas of this plan. The covered porch
could be glazed to form a sun lounge, opening
off both the living bend dining rooms.

Overall Length 57'08"
Overall Width 29'07"
Floor Area 1345 sq.ft.

£G

Additional Options and Services Available. See page 17.

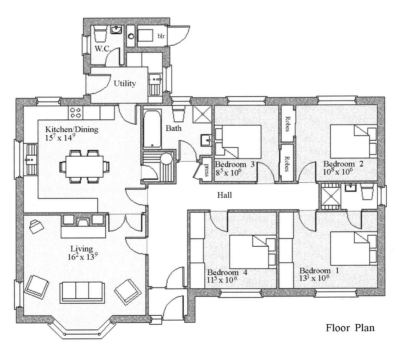

Floor Plan

Overall Length 49'00"
Overall Width 27'02"
Floor Area 1364 sq.ft.

This is an attractive and contemporary bungalow.
A feature to note here is that the fascia runs flush
against the wall with no eaves projection.
The removal of the enclosed porch would make
this design elligible for a house grant.

Construction Costs
For a guideline of costs
in Section A see pages
48 and 49.

Additional Options and Services Available. See page 17.

Two Bedroom

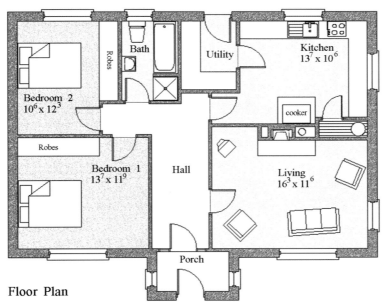

Floor Plan

Bedroom 2
10^6 x 12^3

Robes

Bath

Utility

Kitchen
13^7 x 10^6

cooker

Robes

Bedroom 1
13^7 x 11^9

Hall

Living
16^3 x 11^6

Porch

<u>Plan-A-Home</u>
For a full Architectural
Service. See our advert
inside back pages.

This compact plan exhibits substantial living and
bedroom space. The traditional porch adds flavour
to the overall appearance.

Overall Length 38'05"
Overall Width 31'00"
Floor Area 925 sq.ft.

Additional Options and Services Available. See page 17.

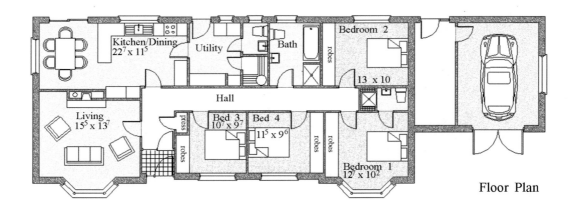

Kitchen/Dining
22⁷ x 11⁵

Utility

Bath

robes

Bedroom 2

13 x 10

Living
15⁵ x 13⁷

press

robes

Hall

Bed 3
10⁷ x 9⁷

Bed 4
11⁵ x 9⁶

robes

robes

Bedroom 1
12⁷ x 10²

Floor Plan

Overall Length	78'04"
Overall Width	26'04"
Floor Area	1503 sq.ft.
Garage	204 sq.ft.

Twin bays are distinctive feature of this balanced facade. The garage annex is shown as separate from the main house but an access through could be formed.

Plan-A-Home
For advice on planning applications.

Additional Options and Services Available. See page 17.

32

Three Bedroom

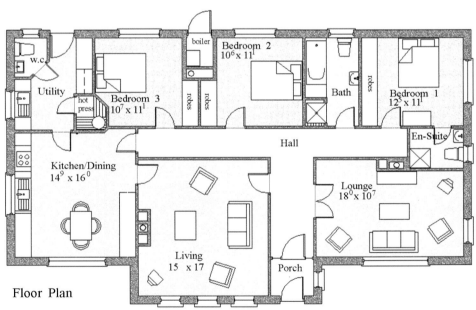

Floor Plan

<hr />

<u>Construction Costs</u>
For a guideline of costs
in Section A see pages
48 and 49.

This is an example of a dwelling that incorporates
two sitting room type spaces. These are simply
distinguished by differences in glazing and door
types used.

Overall Length 57'01"
Overall Width 34'06"
Floor Area 1621 sq.ft.

Additional Options and Services Available. See page 17.

Three Bedroom

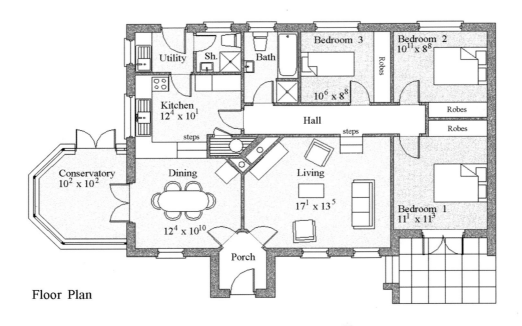

Floor Plan

Conservatory
10^2 x 10^2

Dining
12^4 x 10^{10}

Porch

Living
17^1 x 13^5

Bedroom 1
11^1 x 11^3

Utility

Sh.

Bath

Bedroom 3

Bedroom 2
10^{11} x 8^8

Kitchen
12^4 x 10^1

steps

Hall

steps

Robes

Robes

Robes

10^6 x 8^8

Overall Length 43'01"
Overall Width 28'02"
Floor Area 1190 sq.ft.

A marriage of contemporary and vernacular elements
contrasted in the glazed conservatory and traditional porch.
One enters straight into the living space of this genial home.

Construction Costs
For a guideline of costs
in Section A see pages
48 and 49.

£G

Additional Options and Services Available. See page 17.

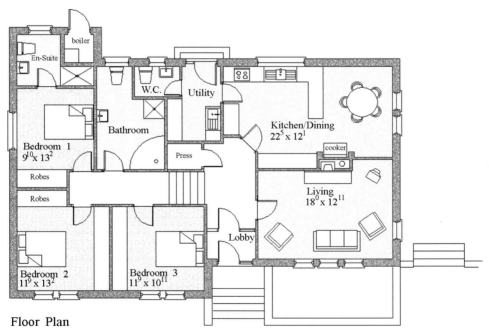

Floor Plan

Plan-A-Home
Provide Mortgage
supervision

A distinctive split level structure, the interesting facade
is notable for its marriage of stone and render.
Internally the step in plan defines the sleeping
accommodation from the more public living areas.

Overall Length 50'00"
Overall Width 27'04"
Floor Area 1345 sq.ft.

Additional Options and Services Available. See page 17.

Three Bedroom

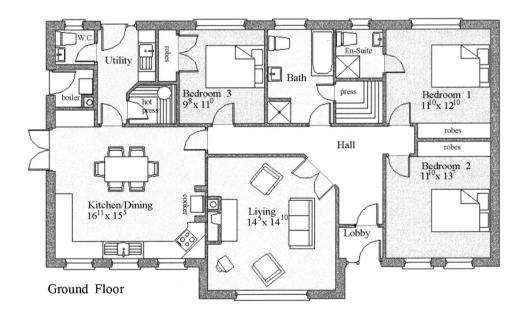

Ground Floor

Overall Length 51'00"
Overall Width 32'00"
Floor Area 1345 sq.ft.

Parapet walls are comon to vernacular housing in many areas of the country. Traditional detailing blended with modern design can be distinctive and afford a sense of identity to a new dwelling.

<u>Plan-A-Home</u>
For complete site survey and analysis.

Additional Options and Services Available. See page 17.

Three Bedroom

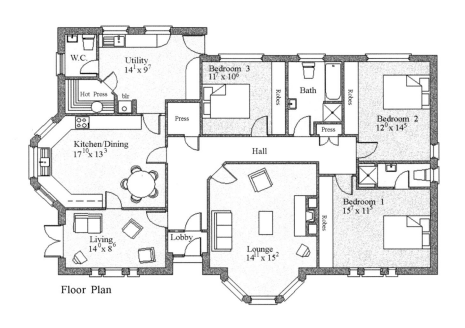

Floor Plan

Construction Costs
For a guideline of costs in Section A see pages 48 and 49.

The formation of the kitchen within the bay is an appealing and practical use of space. This plan is also notable for its spacious utility room and its adaptability.

Overall Length 53'00"
Overall Width 31'11"
Floor Area 1665 sq.ft.

For Metric/Imperial conversion table see page 17.

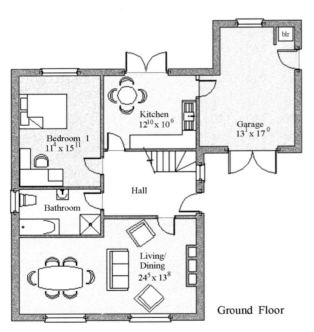

Ground Floor

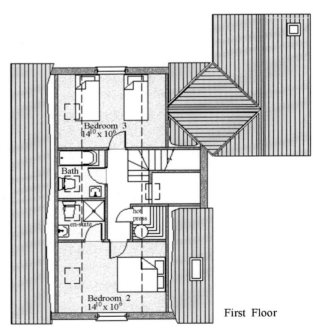

First Floor

Overall Length	36'01"
Overall Width	26'05"
Ground Floor	833 sq.ft.
First Floor	506 sq.ft.
Floor Area	1339 sq.ft.

Designs 5019 & 5020 are variations on a similar plan type. This is a conventional dormer dwelling with bedrooms upstairs. The garage could easily convert to extend the kitchen and form a utility room.

Construction Costs
For a guideline of costs in Section A see pages 48 and 49.

Additional Options and Services Available. See page 17.

Three Bedroom

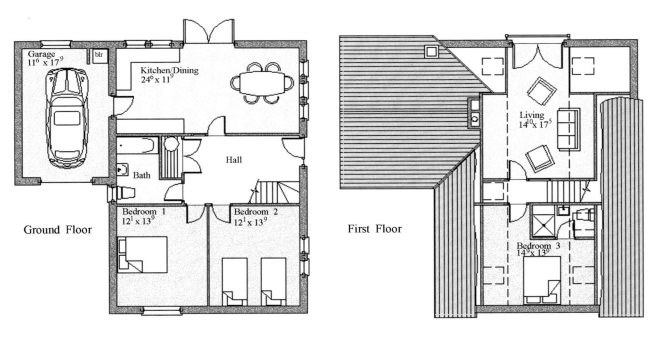

Ground Floor

Garage
11⁶ x 17⁹

blr

Kitchen/Dining
24⁶ x 11⁹

Hall

Bath

Bedroom 1
12¹ x 13⁹

Bedroom 2
12¹ x 13⁹

First Floor

Living
14¹⁰ x 17⁵

Bedroom 3
14⁹ x 13⁹

Plan-A-Home
supply fully computer
generated drawings.

A reversal of the traditional layout. The living room is
located upstairs with a walkway opening up onto the
kitchen and dining room below. A very distinctive
look is achieved by use of contrasting colour in the
wall and frame finishes.

Overall Length	37'04"
Overall Width	26'05"
Ground Floor	866 sq.ft.
First Floor	479 sq.ft.
Floor Area	1345 sq.ft.

Additional Options and Services Available. See page 17.

Four Bedroom

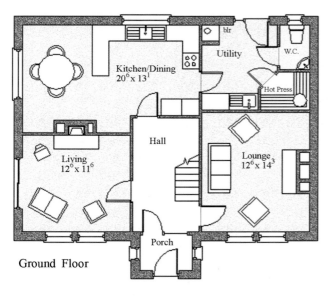

Ground Floor

Kitchen/Dining
20^6 x 13^1

Utility

blr

W.C.

Hot Press

Living
12^6 x 11^6

Hall

Lounge
12^6 x 14^3

Porch

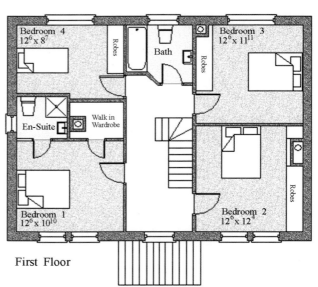

First Floor

Bedroom 4
12^6 x 8^7

Robes

Bath

Robes

Bedroom 3
12^6 x 11^{11}

En-Suite

Walk in
Wardrobe

Bedroom 1
12^6 x 10^{10}

Bedroom 2
12^6 x 12^4

Robes

Overall Length	35'04''
Overall Width	27'00''
Ground Floor	860 sq.ft.
First Floor	830 sq.ft.
Floor Area	1690 sq.ft.

This is a fine illustration of how a simple, elegant form can benefit from attention to material finish and detailing.

Plan-A-Home
Have an in-house bureau supplying computer generated models.

Additional Options and Services Available. See page 17.

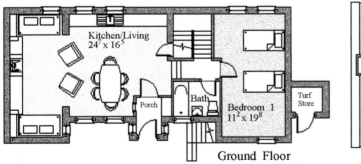

Kitchen/Living
24^7 x 16^5

Porch | Bath

Bedroom 1
11^2 x 19^8

Turf Store

Ground Floor

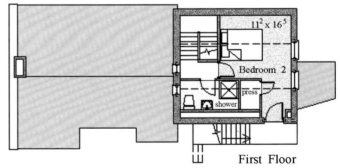

11^2 x 16^5

Bedroom 2

press

shower

First Floor

<u>Construction Costs</u>
For a guideline of costs
in Section A see pages
48 and 49.

A thatched cottage modelled on a vernacular time.
The traditional bed 'outshot' and gable hearth
are the focus of the living space.

Overall Length	44'11"
Overall Width	21'08"
Ground Floor	775 sq.ft.
First Floor	262 sq.ft.
Floor Area	1037 sq.ft.

£G

Additional Options and Services Available. See page 17.

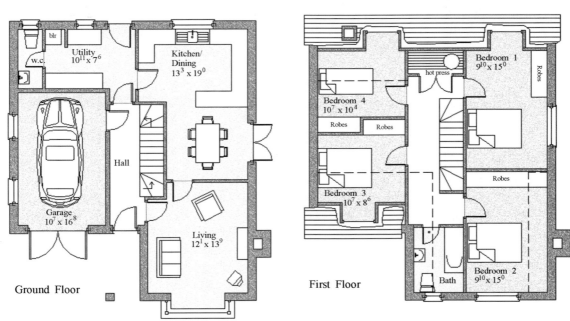

Ground Floor

- blr
- w.c.
- Utility 10¹¹ x 7⁶
- Kitchen/Dining 13³ x 19⁰
- Hall
- Garage 10⁷ x 16⁸
- Living 12¹ x 13⁹

First Floor

- Bedroom 4 10⁷ x 10⁴
- Robes
- Robes
- hot press
- Bedroom 1 9¹⁰ x 15⁰
- Robes
- Bedroom 3 10⁷ x 8⁶
- Robes
- Bath
- Bedroom 2 9¹⁰ x 15⁰

Overall Length	29'10"
Overall Width	35'02"
Ground Floor	601 sq.ft.
First Floor	740 sq.ft.
Floor Area	1341 sq.ft.

A combination of brick, tile and timber finish affords a warm and colourful appearance to this house. Grey leading to the dormer window also provides an attractive maintenance free finish.

Construction Costs
For a guideline of costs in Section A see pages 48 and 49.

£G

Additional Options and Services Available. See page 17.

Four Bedroom

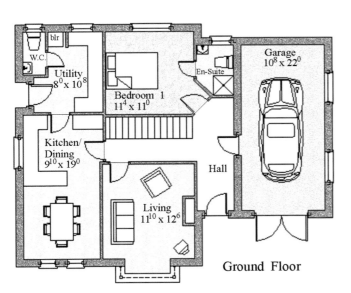

Ground Floor

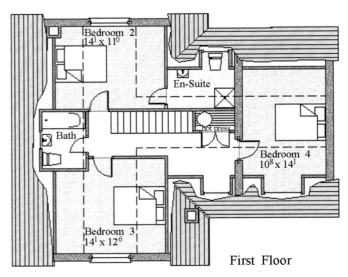

First Floor

Plain clay tile is the illustrated roof finish shown here,
although the design will lend itself to other
material finishes.

Overall Length	40'08"
Overall Width	32'00"
Ground Floor	775 sq.ft.
First Floor	742 sq.ft.
Floor Area	1517 sq.ft.

For metric/imperial conversion table see page 17.

Three Bedroom

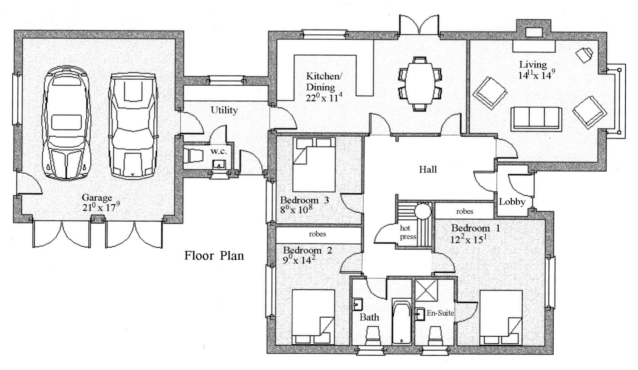

Floor Plan

| Garage 21⁰ x 17⁹ |
| Utility |
| w.c. |
| Kitchen/Dining 22⁰ x 11⁴ |
| Living 14¹¹ x 14⁹ |
| Hall |
| Lobby |
| Bedroom 3 8⁶ x 10⁸ |
| robes |
| hot press |
| robes |
| Bedroom 1 12² x 15¹ |
| Bedroom 2 9⁰ x 14² |
| Bath |
| En-Suite |

Overall Length	68'05"
Overall Width	38'09"
Floor Area	1345 sq.ft.
Garage	377 sq.ft.

All plans are open to interpretation and change both in relation to the site and your needs. This plan is a good example of how an idea may be adapted. The garage could be utilised as living space or rooms could be created within the roofspace.

Plan-A-Home
Have offices in Cork, Dublin, Donegal and Galway. See inside back pages for de-

Additional Options and Services Available. See page 17.

Two Bedroom

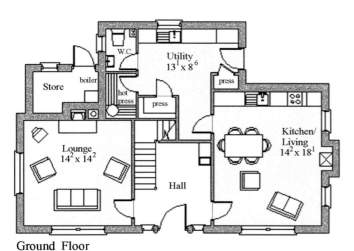

Ground Floor

Store

boiler

W.C.

Utility
13^1 x 8^6

hot press

press

press

Lounge
14^2 x 14^2

Hall

Kitchen/
Living
14^2 x 18^1

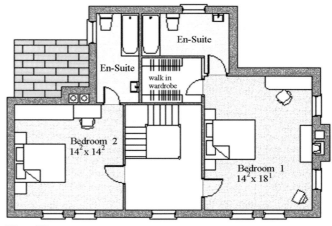

First Floor

En-Suite

En-Suite

walk in wardrobe

Bedroom 2
14^2 x 14^2

Bedroom 1
14^2 x 18^1

<u>Construction Costs</u>
For a guideline of costs in Section A see pages 48 and 49.

Reminiscent of the Georgian entrance, the doorway is a focal point of this facade. Internally, planning is generous and ramifications are possible.

Overall Length	40'10"
Overall Width	28'04"
Ground Floor	868 sq.ft.
First Floor	806 sq.ft.
Floor Area	1674 sq.ft.

Additional Options and Services Available. See page 17.

Two Bedroom

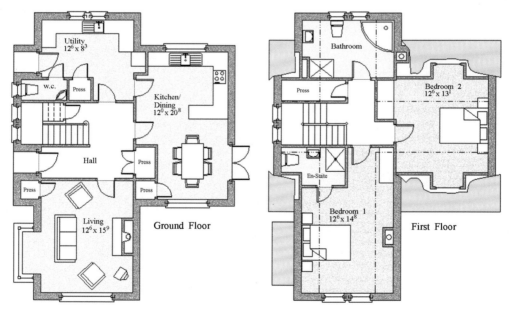

Utility
12⁶ x 8³

w.c.   Press

Kitchen/
Dining
12⁶ x 20⁸

Hall   Press

Press   Press

Living
12⁶ x 15⁹   Ground Floor

Bathroom

Press

Bedroom 2
12⁶ x 13¹

En-Suite

Bedroom 1
12⁶ x 14⁸   First Floor

Overall Length	30'00"
Overall Width	40'04"
Ground Floor	790 sq.ft.
First Floor	694 sq.ft.
Floor Area	1484 sq.ft.

This engaging house is notable for its subtle variation in window and door types. The powder blue render is a good illustration of how colour can be used to dramatic effect.

Construction Costs
For a guideline of costs in Section A see pages 48 and 49.

Additional Options and Services Available. See page 17.

Four Bedroom

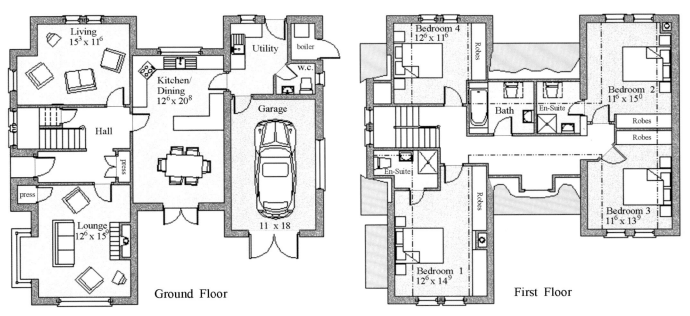

Ground Floor

First Floor

This is a variation of design 5027. The change in external
finish makes a marked difference to the overall appearance
of the building. The addition of a garage increases the first
floor area and facilitates extra bedrooms.

Overall Length 42'06"
Overall Width   40'04"
Ground Floor   901 sq.ft.
First Floor   1027 sq.ft.
Floor Area   1928 sq.ft.

Additional Options and Services Available. See page 17.

Construction Costs

Construction costs in each of the stages - A, B and C are based on three different levels of finish. The specification chosen is, in our opinion, somewhat typical of the size of house.

As building costs vary greatly throughout the country our intention is to indicate prices typical for general areas. If you are on the border of the highlighted regions your price will fall somewhere between those given. To help identify projected overall expenditure we have broken the prices into three stages.

Stage A - *Main Structure*

This includes for all works (material and labour) in constructing your house: foundations, walls, roof, plastering, plumbing, electrical and joinery.
See also 'Guideline Specifications' on Page 49.
Houses illustrated with a stone or brick cladding have only been priced for a rendered finish.
For brick cladding add approximately 10% to the figure given under Stage A.
For stone cladding add approximately 20% to the figure given under Stage A.

All costings are based on traditional construction methods (using cavity blockwork walls) and a contract procurement method - employing a contractor through selective tendering rather than utilising direct labour.

The use of timber frame construction as an alternative to blockwork will have negligible cost implications.

Stage B - *Fit Out*

You may have an idea of how much you intend spending on these items. If so you can adjust the figures accordingly.

Items include:
i) sanitary ware, including for all fittings, taps, shower mixers, shower doors and panels.
ii) kitchen and utility units, not kitchen appliances
iii) fireplaces.
iv) wall tiling.
Ranges, stoves and wardrobes are not included.
See also 'Guideline Specifications' on Page 49.

The figure given in Stage B includes for Stages 'A' and 'B'.

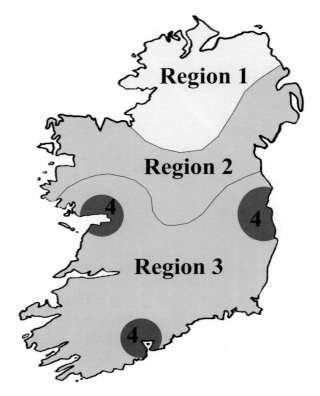

NOTE: Region 4 (areas in red) - It is currently impossible to accurately predict pricing trends in these areas. However, developments in region 4 may increase by up to 10% to 20 % of region 3.
Other cities may also experience similar trends of escalating construction costs.

Stage C - *Site Works*

You may have an idea of how much you intend
This is a provisional amount allowed for all site works and services based on a green field site of approximately half an acre and includes for: footpaths, driveways, sewerage, storm water and water supply. Fencing or boundary walls have not been included in this amount. A serviced site will be less expensive to develope.

The figure given in Stage C includes for Stages 'A', 'B' and 'C'.

KEY

plan	stage	region 1	region 2	region 3
5001	A	77,846	87,188	96,778
	B	88,160	98,740	109,601
	C	96,025	107,549	119,379

To read costings:
1. Refer to plan number - for example 5001.
2. Find your region - e.g. Roscommon is Region 2.
3. The Chart indicates expenditure at Stages outlined i.e.
Shell complete equals Stage A = €87,188 but to complete house to a moving in stage = €107,549.

Guideline Specifications
Section A

Stage A

Roof: Redland concrete tiles.
External Walls: smooth render.
Fascia/soffit: upvc or aluminium.
Windows/external doors: upvc double glazed.
Internal doors: Regency six panel white.
Architrave/skirting: painted softwood.

Stage B

All as detailed on page 48 and including for:
Laminated kitchen/utility units;
1200mm high wall tiling to baths, showers &
W.C.'s;
500mm tiling above worktops;
Decoration to external walls and second fix
joinery.

Stage C

Siteworks as detailed with gravel drive & kerbs.

Please Note:
The prices listed here are for guideline purposes only and are indicative of contract values current in €uro's at Spring 2003.

plan	option	region 1	region 2	region 3
5001	A	77,846	87,188	96,778
	B	88,160	98,740	109,601
	C	96,025	107,549	119,379
5002	A	68,482	76,699	85,136
	B	79,398	88,926	98,708
	C	86,741	97,150	107,837
5003	A	62,735	70,263	77,992
	B	73,198	81,982	91,000
	C	80,638	90,314	100,249
5004	A	58,524	65,547	72,758
	B	66,806	74,823	83,054
	C	74,149	83,047	92,182
5005	A	79,799	89,375	99,207
	B	95,317	106,755	118,499
	C	102,081	114,331	126,907
5006	A	88,220	98,807	109,676
	B	103,414	115,823	128,564
	C	110,755	124,046	137,691
5007	A	84,086	94,176	104,536
	B	99,698	111,661	123,944
	C	107,040	119,885	133,073
5008	A	86,655	97,054	107,729
	B	99,569	111,517	123,784
	C	106,912	119,741	132,913
5009	A	76,265	85,416	94,812
	B	90,999	101,918	113,129
	C	98,341	110,142	122,258
5010	A	83,356	93,356	103,628
	B	98,973	110,850	123,044
	C	106,315	119,073	132,170
5011	A	83,069	93,037	103,272
	B	97,670	109,390	121,423
	C	105,013	117,614	130,552
5012	A	52,558	58,865	65,340
	B	62,692	70,216	77,939
	C	70,034	78,438	87,066

plan	stage	region 1	region 2	region 3
5013	A	94,552	105,898	117,547
	B	107,383	120,269	133,498
	C	114,726	128,493	142,627
5014	A	93,369	104,573	116,076
	B	108,620	121,655	135,037
	C	115,944	129,858	144,142
5015	A	76,974	86,211	95,694
	B	88,457	99,072	109,970
	C	95,800	107,296	119,099
5016	A	81,828	91,647	101,728
	B	95,793	107,288	119,090
	C	102,802	115,138	127,803
5017	A	77,550	86,856	96,411
	B	94,625	105,980	117,638
	C	101,618	113,812	126,331
5018	A	100,581	112,651	125,043
	B	115,347	129,189	143,400
	C	122,689	137,411	152,527
5019	A	91,189	102,131	113,366
	B	105,019	117,621	130,559
	C	112,361	125,845	139,688
5020	A	93,413	104,622	116,130
	B	103,219	115,605	128,322
	C	110,562	123,829	137,450
5021	A	86,169	96,510	107,126
	B	101,051	113,177	125,626
	C	109,244	122,353	135,812
5022	A	84,294	94,409	104,794
	B	95,006	106,406	118,111
	C	102,344	114,625	127,234
5023	A	90,154	100,973	112,080
	B	101,996	114,235	126,801
	C	109,337	122,458	135,928
5024	A	103,607	116,040	128,804
	B	119,372	133,697	148,403
	C	126,713	141,919	157,530
5025	A	105,703	118,388	131,410
	B	118,983	133,261	147,919
	C	126,326	141,485	157,048
5026	A	88,188	98,771	109,636
	B	103,043	115,409	128,104
	C	110,386	123,633	137,232
5027	A	86,317	96,675	107,309
	B	99,820	111,799	124,097
	C	107,163	120,023	133,225
5028	A	119,069	133,357	148,027
	B	135,466	151,722	168,412
	C	142,809	159,946	177,540

kulor Centre

The natural and the traditional in Irish homes

Until very recently crafted and hand-made items of native origin were by in large ignored by the Irish population. Perhaps the new and the unknown seemed so much more attractive than anything that was on offer in this country. Tales of the 'latest thing' abroad, related back home by immigrants and those who had left Ireland to work struck home and the seed was sown; the hand-made and the traditional took a back seat to the imported and the mass produced. Now the tide has begun to turn. There is a definite shift in fashion towards natural fabrics and materials, or perhaps even it could be said that there is a desire to hang onto, moderise and make part of our lives elements from the past that are part of our cultural identity. There is a whole new generation of highly skilled and expertly trained designers working to re-discover and re-invent our material culture in all the design disciplines including textiles, pottery, glass, metalwork and furniture.

Much of current Irish architecture exhibits a coupling of vernacular and contemporary elements. Traditional porches and deep set window reveals marry with dynamic fenestration and are moulded into a congruous whole by using traditional fabric in new and exciting ways.

Many features that were deliberately banished from modern homes because of their 'old-fashionedness' have been re-discovered and implemented, not only because of their simple and pleasing appearance but also for their practical usage.

A revival of the type of fireplace associated with the seanachaí and the storytelling tradition is a reaction to the contemporary gathering around the television instead of the hearth. Nooks and openings are built into the structure of the fireplace to form seating, storage space for logs and lamp holes for candles. The fireplace becomes not only a point of focus for the room, but a useful and welcoming space in its own right.

Variations on the settle bed are also growing in popularity often as a foil to the kitchen range. These can take the form of a timber bench where the seat lifts and storage is provided underneath. The settle could be an attractive option for the holiday home acting

At the heart of our system is all the energy you'll ever need.

REAL FLAME FIRES

COOKING

HOT WATER

TUMBLE DRYING

Calor Home Energy Systems are specifically designed to meet your individual requirements.

In addition to central heating, a Calor Home Energy System can also heat your water, dry your clothes, fuel your cooker, and of course, provide the warmth and cosiness that only a real flame fire can bring to a house.

What's more, because gas is such a clean fuel, there's no need to worry about harmful by-products, which has to be good news for the environment.

With Calor you can control the energy output of your home in a more effective and efficient manner. An extensive range of modern gas appliances can be instantly powered from a single source. There's even a choice of supply options for your convenience.

For information on Calor Home Energy Systems, or a copy of our brochure, phone our sales office on (01) 450 5000.

And discover for yourself why a Calor Home Energy System should be at the heart of your new home.

CALOR GAS
Wherever you live.

Dave & Sue Prickett Furniture

Luckpenny Antiques

Mark Wilkinson Furniture

as comfy, fireside seating during the day and doubling as bed space at night.

Other types of furniture such as the dresser and the wash stand have been updated and in the case of the wash stand 'plumbed' to facilitate the demands of modern living. It may be possible to draw on the skill of a local potter and have a hand-thrown basin instead of the typical characterless sanitary fitting.

A variation on the clevy has also become popular. The clevy was a wooden shelf mounted over the fireside, originally to hold a long spit. After the spit became obsolete, the practice of fixing increasingly ornate clevies purely to display pottery and other ornaments became popular. Deep window reveals add character to a room, framing windows and views accentuating the qualities of light and shadow. A wide window niche can facilitate a seat or workbench. Timber shutters forgo the need for curtaining and maximise the amount of incoming light.

Coupled with native fabrics and textiles these features give a character and essence that is essentially Irish. Tweeds, soft woollen and heavy weave fabrics complement natural timber floor and furniture finish. Natural dyed tweed hung as curtaining can echo and emphasise the dramatic colouring of the scenery beyond.

Irish designers so very often draw on our diverse landscape for inspiration for their work. In finishing our homes we too can make use of the subtle tones blended in nature to dramatic effect in the interiors of our homes. Allow the washed orange and brown from the turf bogs, steel greys and purple heather tones of the mountainside to inspire your choice of fabric, wall and floor coverings.

All around us, be it in the buildings of the past or the ever present landscape there is inspiration to create essentially Irish homes.

Waterford Crystal

Joinery

The first major feature seen by someone stepping through the front door of a house is the hallway. The initial impact generated by a well designed hallway and staircase should not be under emphasised. As the saying goes, first impressions are lasting.

The staircase has often been a missed opportunity, viewed purely as a means of linking floors together. An impressive and attractive staircase can be created at relatively little extra cost, to provide a key benefit and extra selling features.

The enormous choices available include many different timbers, straight-grained and even textured softwoods. They are ideal for complementing country style and contemporary interiors, whilst mahogany and oak suit the more traditional and classical interior schemes.

Spindle styles range from simple elegance to more ornate designs. Interesting stair designs can be created using quarter and half landings. Winders and accessories such as bullnose treads and different handrail systems also allow different effects to be achieved.

The more reputable joinery companies provide a high level of support and assistance on design and construction. Skirting boards may be complemented by a range of elegant architraves which can be teamed with corner blocks to create a distinctive finish to doorways and windows.

There is a large selection of dado rails from the Victorian, Edwardian and Regency periods, providing the opportunity to create striking borders and allowing exciting changes of wall colour or texture. Combined with picture rail and cornice, an elegant individual co-ordinated look is easily achieved by the thoughtful planner.

Crown/Berger

Richard Burbidge Ireland Ltd

Richard Burbidge Ireland Ltd

Richard Burbidge Ireland Ltd

Wickanders

Timber Flooring

To many of us timber floors raise memories of hard work and difficulties in maintenance. But today's surface coatings have removed the wax polishing drudge and the choice and range of specially prepared hardwoods has given a new life to what is a very old and well tried feature.

Where cleanliness and hygiene are concerned, not many other floor covering materials can match Oak hardwood floors. There are no fibres to hold dust mites. Have you ever stood in a sunlit, carpeted room, where a vacum cleaner was in use, have you seen the amount of dust being exhausted. The surface of an Oak hardwood floor is very hard and durable, and any dust is removed easily through brushing or vacuming. This has great advantages for people who have dust allergies as their exposure to dust is dramatically reduced.

Parquet is synonymous with hardwoods laid in geometric patterns to achieve a pleasing design that enhances and appears to add to the space in the room. Parquet flooring was developed mainly in northern Europe to decorate large areas and to provide a warmth of atmosphere using exotic timbers from all over the world .

The requirement for a hard-wearing floor led to the development of the wood block that locked together using tongue and groove technique in a herringbone pattern with a thickness of up to 35mm so that when it started to look out of condition it could be planed or sanded to show a new surface. Modern coatings have removed the necessity for this. Nonetheless, the cost and availability of this type of flooring has become quite prohibitive.

Cost consciousness has led to a range of pre-finished floors in plank and tile form. A number of these use timber or other stable supports for the expensive surface layer of hardwood. Pre-finished in the factory, it is lacquered with tough surface coatings to protect from wear and to develop the colour / grain patterns thus providing a surface that is easily maintained.

The cost of timber flooring compared with the life of other floor coverings is more than competitive particularly as there is nothing "as natural as natural timber". A visit to your local architectural salvage professional might unearth some reclaimed boards which look tremendous and create that 'Antique' look.

Marquetry techniques can be used to inlay patterns and motifs into timber floors. These mosaic type designs can be achieved by using different types of wood or stained pieces of timber.

People love the versatility of wooden floors, they can be sanded, painted, stencilled and sealed to give a pleasing if sometimes rather noisy and draughty effect. Use a silk rather than a gloss clear varnish, as the latter will show up every dent and scratch on the surface. But be advised that if it's a quiet, cosy environment you are seeking to create then you will need to compensate with plenty of soft furnishings and rugs.

A professionally laid timber floor complements any form of architecture or interior design, blending with all colours, hard and soft furnishings, transforming a home into a palace of elegance.

Ronseal Paints

Junkers/Brooks Thomas

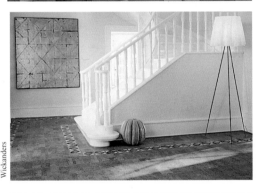

Wickanders

oakleaf Conservatories

Junkers/Brooks Thomas

Alternative Floor Finishes

The next point to bear in mind is how many people are going to use the area on a regular basis? It is important to know the composition of the floor, whether wood or concrete, as this may have a very strong bearing on the suitability of your chosen flooring material.

Wooden, chipboard or MDF floors have a certain amount of resilience and spring in them and this very flexibility makes them an excellent base on which to fit carpet or carpet tiles; rugs; coir matting; cork tiles; parquet wood blocks and vinyl - sheet or tile.

Concrete has no give whatsoever and is best covered in carpet or carpet tiles, lino, coir matting, and of course, ceramic or quarry tiles.

Vinyl must be laid on an even subfloor otherwise joints between the floor boards or panels may be visible or cause cracking in the surface material. Vinyl is available in a wide range of colours and finishes and is extremely durable..

In Ireland we often opt for carpet or rugs because they are warmer underfoot and feel good to walk upon. Carpet, however, does need careful maintenance. A weekly vacuum and light daily sweep with a sweeping brush or carpet sweeper is quite sufficient, when allied to spot-cleaning of stains.

Ceramic and quarry floor tiles are basic and utilitarian but in very recent times an amazing interest in tiling has been kindled. Today the variety of floor tiles is vast. Plain and patterned, costly or inexpensive, the choice is yours. Many wooden floors are unsuitable for quarry or ceramic tiles and those that are suitable require a good sub-suspended plywood floor on which to fix the tiles - otherwise, the spring in the floor will crack the tile cement and then the tiles!

Coir and sisal although not cheap offer two natural alternatives. Sisal is a hard fibre made from the leaves of the sisalana plant, grown mainly in Haiti and Eastern Africa. Coir is an elastic fibre made from Coconut husks in the islands of the southwestern coast of India. Both have rich colours and are deep textured which produces a warm atmosphere in the home. As floor coverings they are very insulative against cold, moisture and sound

Leading the way in the built environment

AutoCAD AEC

30 40 50 60

The industry standard by which others are measured

AutoCAD AEC Release 5.1 with Annotation Manager, linking to NBS' Specification Manager and Barbour Index's Construction expert, is the latest version of the market leading 2D and 3D drafting and design software for UK architectural, construction and built environment applications. This industry standard software meets the demand for greater sophistication and ease of use and extends its functionality to related fields such as building services, facilities management, civil engineering, architecture and construction, together with house building ... placing AutoCAD AEC at the heart of design for the built environment.

To discover how AutoCAD AEC 5.1 could fit into your organisation call CADCO on:

Northern Ireland: 0645 123 539
Republic of Ireland: 1890 501 414
(All calls at local rate)

Website: **www.cadco.ie**

CADCO
CAD • EDM • TRAINING

Autodesk®

DESIGN YOUR WORLD

Does your software measure up to AutoCAD AEC?

but they hate stains like ink or red wine. Linoleum is a natural material, experiencing a revival and made from, amongst other ingredients, crushed cork - a particular tree bark. It is extremely durable and safe and unless subject to intense heat or cold will last a very long time. It is available in an array of colours and finishes but does require a skilled fitter to see it at its best.

Whatever you choose, think about it carefully and don't be rushed into making a decision. Most flooring is expensive and should last a long time so whatever you choose you'll probably be looking at it for some time.

HGW/Dulux

Beam

V'Soske Joyce

Tilesavers

WHO WE ARE

HMG Associates & CMG, Architects
Founded in 1980 we have since grown into a nationwide multi disciplinary practice with a network of offices in Letterkenny, Cork. Galway, Carlow and Moville.

Our success is driven by our determination and enthusiasm to deliver creative functional solutions to the highest standard on time and within budget

The company has extensive experience of a wide variety of projects both in private and public sectors of all scales and degrees of complexity.

Our style is one of listening and acting as the "hub" in forming a cohesive working partnership with clients, contractors, consultants and the needs of the built environment.

WHY HMG & CMG

Due to our multi disciplinary structure we provide you with a single point of reference for the various consultants required to develop and complete your project.

We advise and assist on all feasibility aspects of your proposal including viability, location, cost, business plan, loans, grant aid availability, etc., by carefully listening to and enthusiastically responding to your needs.

We can confidently assure you, through our team of experienced professionals that we have the necessary skills and procedures to achieve your goals from project inception through brief development, sketch and detailed design.

See inside back cover for office locations and details

Smallbone

Kitchens

The smallest of details can make a considerable difference in making time spent in the kitchen into either a joy or a chore. While it's simple enough to replace a kettle or move a toaster closer to the bread bin, larger accessories such as hobs, ovens and freezers are investments that prove that compromising on quality is expensive in the long run. Quality design has as much to do with being aesthetically pleasing as ensuring smooth performance. A kitchen can be destroyed by the discordant note of mismatched dimensions, non-coordinated colours or ill-conceived variations in textures.

When it comes to kitchens and kitchen accessories it is essential to take a total approach. The very individual requirements must be studied and met both in terms of visual design and in the performance and range of facilities available. All fitted appliances should be fully integrated into the overall design theme selected for the kitchen. Door panels identical to, or coordinating with, the colour scheme and dimensions of the kitchen are fitted to the appliance door, remaining flush with the rest of the kitchen units. This not only means the end of unattractive exposed appliances such as washing machines but also gives the impression of greater space. The professional

Woodstock Furniture

kitchen designer optimises available space by advising on where to install kitchen appliances, ensuring the kitchen is not merely a showpiece but a practical and functional workroom. For instance the kitchen may incorporate a vacuum cleaner cupboard with extra storage space to accommodate such items as a sewing machine or perhaps a base unit specially designed for hanging clothes.

These represent only a small selection of the quiet revolution that has taken place in kitchen and accessories design over the last two decades. Lifestyle changes mean that today's client expects far more from the kitchen than ever before. Instant energy- efficient performance is expected and top quality results demanded. People no longer want to wait for a repairman to call.

Manufacturers' reputations stand or fall on performance. Cleaning - a time consuming exercise in the past - has also become a quick and easy task now with simple to clean surfaces and features such as detachable shelves and doors, leaving no awkward nooks and crannies that used to be so difficult to get at. Self-cleaning ovens are another godsend to busy cooks as are fast-freeze trays for the rapid freezing of such items as fruit.

Siematic/Houseworks

The options for kitchen design are limitless but the success of any kitchen depends entirely on the amount of thought and time invested in the planning stage, and integrating these requirements with the ultimate design to create a kitchen that will be a true centre in the home for lifetimes to come.

Poggenphol

Helen O'Connor. *Homemaker.*

It's all about efficiency: *Doing a task with the minimum effort
for the maximum results.
It's my Stanley - this heart of the home
around which everything revolves. It makes the house look good
and seem cosy in the middle of winter, but stays cool all Summer.*

IT'S **ALL**
ABOUT
efficiency

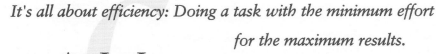

*It sits there almost guarding the family,
cooking away quietly, gently spreading
warmth through the house.*

*The cast iron oven is incredibly efficient:
It's sealed so that the moisture and flavour stays where it belongs, while the iron frame heats up to cook evenly.
Then there's the twin burners: One for heating and hot water. One for cooking. Both independent,
both on timers, both thermostatically controlled, both very efficient.*

*And while Stanley cooks, I clean with all that hot water. Unless it's Saturday,
in which case Stanley cooks while He cleans.
Yes it takes Him a whole day, but then I'm not there to show Him
how to do it efficiently...*

Waterford Stanley. All about the home.

A Waterford Stanley Range. For cooking, central heating and hot water in gas, oil or solid fuel.

Buyer Be Aware

Read any article about fitted kitchens and you will find statements such as: dream kitchen; handcrafted; solid oak; attention to detail, and so on. Don't let terms like these impress you. The main ingredients in a typical kitchen, no matter how much you pay for it, are chipboard, hardboard, and solid timber. A typical Solid Oak Kitchen will have (in board square feet) 85% chipboard|hardboard in the carcase and 15% solid Oak in the doors.

It is possible to get a dream kitchen but hand-crafted ones are few and far between, as most necessary work on an average kitchen can be done better by machine. The lifespan of a kitchen depends on the quality of the materials used, method of manufacture and the way it is fitted. As chipboard is the main ingredient, it is very important that it is of high quality and, more importantly, that it is machined and edged properly. All edges should be sealed with edging tape, even the ones that are not seen, as this prevents them absorbing moisture. Since most of the doors used by kitchen manufacturers are brought in from specialist door manufacturers, the quality is usually assured. However, in the case of solid timber doors, the polishing sometimes leaves a lot to be desired. If a door is not sanded well between coats of sealants and lacquers it will be difficult to clean.

When buying a kitchen you should decide on how much money you have to spend and then shop around for the best buy. On finding one you like the following relevant questions should be asked:

Do the floor cabinets have legs on them?
Do they have a ledge to support the gable of the cabinet?
(It is very important that they have this ledge otherwise the floor to gable fitting is taking the whole weight).
Are the legs metal or plastic?
(Metal legs are stronger than plastic).
What guarantee is given and is it in writing?
Do they make the doors or are they bought in? Do they stain and lacquer the door and endpanels themselves?
Are the end panels melamine or real wood veneer?
(Veneer is best but more expensive).
Are the shelves adjustable and the longer ones supported in the centre to prevent sagging?
Does the worktop have a water safe edge?
Is the cornice and light pelmet solid timber or MDF?

Newcastle Furniture

(It should be solid).
What thickness is the chipboard in the carcase?
(This should not be less than 16mm, preferably 18mm.).
What way are the cabinet doors put together are they KD fittings or wood dowels?
Is there a quality control system in stock?
Have their kitchens undergone independent testing?
(Check details).
When ordering materials do they specify the quality they require?
Do they check on the delivery of goods that they are up to the standard ordered?
Is there a contract form to be signed?

Don't let all these questions put you off. Any manufacturer who thinks quality will welcome them, even if they can't answer positively to them all. The answer to the first two questions should be yes, even on the cheapest kitchen you can buy. Check for yourself the thickness of the cupboard, the drawers, hinges and the shelf supports. Also, if the doors are solid timber, slide your fingers around the edges of the centre panel - this should be smooth to the touch. But most important, check out the person you are dealing with. Remember, you can trade in your car if you are not happy with it; have a bad quality kitchen fitted and you are stuck with it.

AGA Campbell & Cooke

Ranges

However appealing you might find the idea of a traditional farmhouse kitchen, it it unlikely that you will want to cope with a traditional farmhouse inglenook fire, complete with stockpot, or a black leaded range. Happily, you can combine traditional looks with efficient performance. Ranges and stoves now mix rustic appeal with modern needs and can be fuelled by gas, electricity, LPG, wood or solid fuel. Running costs are reasonable - especially if you also use it for hot water.

Most manufacturers provide a dual system which can provide for both cooking and heating your choice very much depends on your requirements such as regular use for cooking high demand for domestic not water, room heating or aesthetics, if you wish to create a focal point within a room

Cooking on this type of appliance means making some changes. Most new users adapt well. All manufacturers supply recipe books and hold frequent demonstrations at stockists and at shows. You will need new pans - to

work well, utensils must have a totally flat, heavy base. Ranges don't of course, have grills. Chops, bacon , sausages, etc. can be cooked in the top oven. Toast is cooked on the hot plate with the bread held in wire mesh grippers, available from manufacturers. Steaks and fish can be done in the same way. Heavy insulation means that the range won't make the kitchen too hot in the summer, so it can be left working all the year round. Central heating ranges do have a 'hot water only' option. Some cooks insist on a second electric single oven, but this isn't necessary. A microwave is the only extra you will really need.

Your choice of appliance may also be governed by how it is going to look. Colour choice is very much up to the individual. The stove can be built into a decorative surrounding and this can be used in a practical way as well, with built in niches or shelves, for cooking utensils or ornaments. A stove may also be built into a run of kitchen units.

Very often the decision to choose a range is influenced by a past association with a traditional or farming background. You may find that a small stove (of the type illustrated on Page 171) without hotplates or cooking facilities is more appropriate to your needs, they are much less bulky and can match the heating capacity of the traditional range.

The dimensions of your kitchen and the overall size of your house may be the most important consideration governing your choice.

Your architect and local heating engineer will discuss all the options with you and assist in making the final choice.

Waterford Stanley

AGA Campbell & Cooke

Fenton Fires

Fireplaces

More and more people are learning daily that an open fire is not just the most satisfying way of warming oneself and one's home, but that it brings to a room a unique range of soft, glowing colour creating an atmosphere that no other form of heating can emulate.

It is for these very reasons that a real fire deserves a really good fireplace, a fireplace that complements and enhances its appeal, a fireplace that looks as good in summer without a fire as it does in winter with. Well designed and superbly crafted, your fireplace can be the most striking and attractive feature of the room, both distinctive and harmonious. Using Ireland's many craftsmen in this field will ensure your fireplace will be the focus of your home.

There are so many styles and designs of fireplaces available on the Irish market today that the customer might feel spoiled for choice. Present day fireplaces demonstrate how creative use of traditional and modern materials, combined with excellence of design and craftsmanship, can create

something which is totally in keeping with your room. In effect, one can have a fireplace designed exclusively to suit their own interior for little more than the cost of a decent fireside chair.

When deciding on a fireplace for your home be sure to take into account the type of open fire or room heater you have (or are going to have) in the new fireplace. In doing this you will be influenced in the style of fireplace and choice of material which will best fit, which you like and which suits your room. Ceramic tiles have long been a popular material. Easy to clean and capable of immense variation, they have developed still further in recent years. Briquettes come in a variety of forms - from the traditional warmth of red sandfaced to the more delicate appeal of riven marble or stone. Stone and slate give a natural appearance to your fireplace. For hearth slabs and facings, slate is the ideal material, while stone is very versatile. Natural or reconstructed stone can be polished, tooled or riven in a variety of modern designs. Metal is a perfect medium for fireplaces. Bronze, copper, brass, cast-iron and stainless steel not only complement and reflect the beauty of a real fire, but they are also durable, heat-resistant, and highly decorative.

Marble is one of the most beautiful of all natural materials.
Wood, of course, is as naturally appealing as the fire itself. From warm mellow oak and polished walnut to traditional pine and painted white wood

Yes, the choice is extensive and many will find it difficult to decide on material, style or design to suit their own home but luckily most manufacturers and showrooms have technical staff on hand to assist in this area.

Browsing amidst a wide range of styles and designs is recommended - it will spark ideas, stimulate fresh thoughts on your fireplace and what is the most suitable for your requirements.

Today's fireplaces are a combination of traditional appeal and modern technology. Together they improve the quality of life.

Brassington

Morso

Jacuzzi/CM Marketing

Bathrooms

More than ever, bathrooms are an expression of character
The suite is the starting point for determining how the entire room will look, its colour, shape and the number of pieces - whether it includes a bidet and matching shower tray, for example - are paramount.

Pretty decorated suites can create a 'country cottage' feel which can
be emphasised with matching tiles, wallpaper borders and floor coverings; a dramatic, sophisticated look can be achieved by the many period suites on the market which echo the Edwardian, Victorian and the Art Deco eras; the modern streamlined contours of many contemporary designs with their cleverly concealed plumbing, offer a simple, pleasing alternative which will fit into most homes.

However, the first step to take when planning any change is to assemble all the available literature. This will enable you to assess the range of products on the market.
Some view the bathroom as a place to relax and dream, others simply look upon it as a functional room, whilst others aim to give it a

"sporty" feel. In fact there is a range of equipment available for the bathroom which would not look out of place in a gym.

For those who do like to wallow there is a range of luxury baths on the market, including circular and corner tubs large enough for two, and, of course, Airbath systems are particularly novel. They blow pre-warmed air through a series of jets in the base of the bath and often have an electronic wave motion selector for local and full massage settings.

Although corner or circular baths create dramatic visual impact, the lack of space in a typical bathroom can be restricting. To address this, some manufacturers have introduced offset corner baths, which require only a little more space than the average rectangular design.
Increasingly popular is bathroom fitted furniture, in which the WC suite and washbasin are set to create cupboards which provide extra storage space for towels, cleaning products and proves invaluable in keeping a bathroom tidy, especially important where the room is on the small side.

Choosing the colour of the bathroom suite is one of the most important decisions for the new house builder. Manufacturers continue to add to the selection, providing numerous alternatives to the ever popular pastel shades, such as peach and grey. The pastel shades create a light, fresh environment whereas a darker colour can be warmer and more dramatic. Colours such as burgundy and dark blue can create an intimate atmosphere and make a room look smaller.

A white suite can be a wise choice as it can easily be matched with floor and wall coverings and may not date as easily as a coloured suite. White suites are available in a wide variety of styles.

Do not neglect taps and mixers. Once again the choice has extended to include modern striking designs or period styles with hand held 'telephone' shower heads for the bath. Choose gold for a touch of luxury, chrome for a clean bold look, and white to give a more modern feel. Coloured tap heads are also available to match the colour of the suite. The choice of bath panels and WC seats can change the character of a room. Many period suites are enhanced by the dramatic use of dark wood panels. And for the finishing touch consider the type of accessories which may best enhance the chosen suite. There are many styles in ceramic, chrome, gold or wood.

Armitage Shanks

Vernon Tutbury

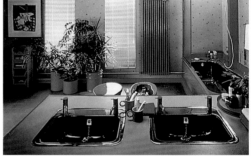

Runtal Radiators

Tylo - Blackchurch Leisure

SHIRES
BATHROOMS

SEE THE BATHROOM COLLECTION
FROM SHIRES

A superb range of exclusive designs, co-ordinated suites,
super luxury baths, showers and shower trays,
fine quality taps and mixers.

SHIRES IRELAND LIMITED, BROOMHILL ROAD, DUBLIN 24.
PH: (01) 4515877   FAX: (01) 4515534

FROM STEAM BATH TO SAUNA
TYLÖ IS ALWAYS ONE STEP AHEAD

TYLÖ leads the field in modern bathing comfort for both private users and public facilities. Tylö products are presented in detail in a number of separate brochures. Please contact Tylö for further information on Tylö Sauna & Steam Rooms, Sauna Heaters & Accessories and Steam Rooms, Sauna Heaters & Accessories and Steam Equipment.

TYLÖ IRE.

**Suncroft, Main Street,
Rathcoole, Co. Dublin
Tel: 01/4589464**

Sanitan

A Little Room for Thought

Accessories are the image creators in the large majority of Irish bathrooms. The furniture for walls and floors of your bathroom should complement the soft accessories for which they have been designed.

If a limited budget has to be adhered to, look simply at paint, and perhaps a toning or contrasting narrow wallpaper border in one of the attractive new ranges available. If you do decide on this, make sure that the ceiling is high enough to take the border. Tiling may not be necessary at all, but if you are installing a shower, either separately or within the bath, it is essential. Make sure to use a thoroughly waterproof grouting. Many a downstairs room can tell a good story so

check your grouting as the months go by. You may need to reseal periodically to be absolutely sure of maintaining waterproof joints along the side of your bath, or the edges of the shower tray.

Soft furnishings are readily available for the bathroom and toilet windows. Let the lovely clear blue sky or summer feature in your bathroom or allow the garden become part of the cloakroom floor. Indeed, it can be fun dreaming up window box ideas for the external sills or planning the flower bed at the end of the garden while drying off behind pretty lace curtains after you've pulled up the blind that you have chosen to match your shower curtain and bathmat set.

Accessories , well, first and foremost a toilet

roll holder, a towel rail of appropriate size, and a toothbrush and tumbler holder. Soap dishes are not always needed but that will depend on the shape of your wash hand basin. You may require shelving, maybe a cabinet and use the shelving for some pretty plates. Could the mirror be round, square, oval or rectangular. Bathrobes too need their space; hang them on the back of the door or feature them on a robe stand in the room. Tiered glass shelving can look very smart. Will there be room for a chair?

Sort your thoughts clearly first, browse through some magazines, enjoy the moment because the time is coming now to see what is available in the shops!

Pipe Dreams

Shires Ireland Ltd

Shires Ireland Ltd

LIGHTING

It is impossible to recreate the fluid quality of natural light. The sun rises in the morning and sets in the evening and from dawn until dusk we are bathed in a myriad of colour and shade. It is for this very reason that we must strive to create lighting effects which are tailored to individual spaces and the demands of the activity that these spaces serve. If the sun was to shine at a constant level from a constant location we would observe very little visible change in the levels of light in the environment around us. We would most likely find this very dull. The same reasoning would therefore point to the fact that if a light source is placed in a room, day in and day out shining at a constant level and from a constant location that the occupant of that room would find it mundane. This is however how most of us choose to light the rooms in our homes.

Practical Needs

The best starting point when considering lighting for your home is to consider the practical needs. Are there particular areas of the kitchen that will need lighting either over work surfaces or the hob top.? What is the best location for your desk and can you have a fixed light fitting or should you allow a socket for a free-standing desk light?

Effect

Once you have decided exactly where direct sources of light are necessary you can start to think about what type of effects you would like to achieve in each room in your home. Shop, Restaurants and other public buildings can provide you with ideas for lighting effects that you can implement in the home. Magazines, books and lighting guides are all also good sources for ideas and usually have illustrations of rooms with specific types of lighting.

General

All spaces require artificial lighting even if you do not have a specific task or purpose in mind. Stairwells should be well-lit for safety purposes and hallways to make them more welcoming to visitors. Use lighting as a way of giving a room its own identity by considering it in the same way that you would approach choosing a wallpaper or a fabric. Different types of light-bulbs give different qualities of light and these will have varying effects on the appearance of fabrics, wall finishes and upholstery.

Phillips Lighting

Planning

Lighting should really be considered at a planning stage. All too often it is a last minute decision or something that is left out to make the budget stretch that little bit further. Do not fall into the later date trap. It is much better to allow provision for lighting during the building process otherwise inevitably the work is never completed. It is also more satisfactory from the electrician and plasterer's points of view as wiring and making good can be completed much more easily while building work is still going on. If lighting is planned for at an early stage it need not be expensive to achieve an interesting effect. The architect will be able to discuss ideas with you.

Types of Light Fitting

Overhead Lights

These provide an illusion of space and provide good general lighting. It is probably a good idea to use this type of lighting in conjunction with other fittings if you want to be able to create mood at other times. A dimmer switch can also be used to advantage in conjunction with this type of fitting.

Pendant Lights

This type of fixture is suspended from the ceiling. Pendant lights should be positioned carefully so that they do not hang at eye level and cause discomfort to those using the room. It is also important that they do not interfere with circulation or the positioning of furniture. An adjustable version of this fitting can be put to good use over a dining room table.

Downlights

Downlights can be recessed into the ceiling or surface mounted. The effects achievable will vary depending on the type of fitting and the bulb used. Some of the smaller fittings have the advantage of being unobtrusive. Downlights can be used in all three situations mentioned: for effect, to provide light for a specific task and as a general light source. Downlights are also available on tracking which allows the position of the fitting to be adjusted as needed.

Uplights

These can be wall mounted or free-standing. Light is directed up and reflects off the ceiling. Uplighting is effective as background lighting but is not suitable for working under. Uplights are inexpensive and come in a wide variety of styles. They can be used to dramatic effect but have the disadvantage of highlighting plaster defects

Dave & Sue Prickett Furniture

Junkers/Brooks Thomas

Baukreacht

Philips Lighting

 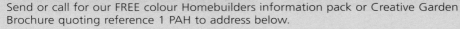

LIGHT SOURCES

TYPE	CHARACTERISTICS	USAGE
Tungsten	Yellow in colour, intensity depends on wattage. Often silvered to reduce glare.	Table Lamps and Hanging Fixtures
Halogen (combination of tungsten and halogen)	Clear white light generating a specific wash or spot of light depending on type.	Effective in uplights
Low-voltage Halogen	Clean sparkling light, fittings are small and discreet.	Successful in shops, may need to reduce glare for home use.
Fluorescent	Usually tubular in shape, with box type diffuser, cast a green tone.	Associated with school and office environments. Can be successful if used as concealed or indirect lighting.
Compact Fluorescent Lamps (CFL)	Energy saving tubular form, less even light than tungsten or halogen.	Use in place of traditional tungsten, they cost more but last longer.

Things to Avoid

- Spotlighting for effect can be distracting. Be careful not to over do it, lighting is only ever as interesting as the object that it is illuminating.
- Be careful not to position a light source directly behind where someone is intended to sit, the face of the person sitting will be difficult to see as they will appear in silhouette and this could make conversation difficult.
- Blocking out Natural Light. Be aware that the highest concentration of light enters through the upper section of a window. Curtains and pelmets should be positioned so that they do not block out this light.

Useful Hints

- Picture lights work well in areas such as hallways where you may wish to display pictures or family photographs.
- A mixture of fittings provides a more individual approach to lighting rather than having all fittings identically matched.
- Wire a socket to the main switch panel in the room, so that a free standing lamp can be switched on as you enter the room to create a softer effect.
- Make use of Dimmer Switches.
- Position plants in front of a window to act as a filter for incoming sunlight, this gives an easy quality of light. A plant placed in front of an artificial light source can also create a dramatic effect.
- Use mirrors to reflect both natural and artificial light within a room.
- Always use a fully accredited electrician to carry out wiring and other electrical works. Your safety is a priority.

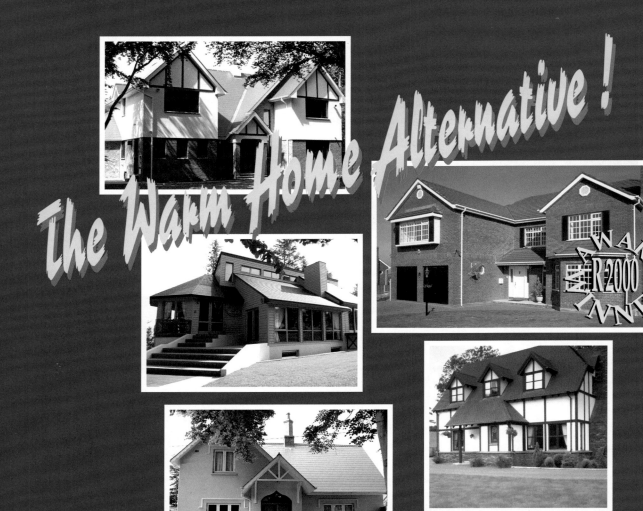

Timber Frame Construction - The warm home alternative

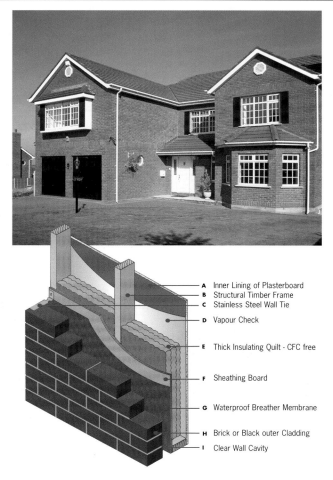

- **A** Inner Lining of Plasterboard
- **B** Structural Timber Frame
- **C** Stainless Steel Wall Tie
- **D** Vapour Check
- **E** Thick Insulating Quilt - CFC free
- **F** Sheathing Board
- **G** Waterproof Breather Membrane
- **H** Brick or Black outer Cladding
- **I** Clear Wall Cavity

Timber Frame as a method of building is not new. It is the most commonly used form of construction in the Western world. It is generally known that approximately 95% of all homes built in North America and Scandinavia are of Timber Frame construction. However, these statistics do not show the real extent of this method of building. Timber Frame accounts for 70% of construction in the developed nations of the world, from countries as warm as Australia to countries as cold and as wet as Scotland, where over 50% of all residential construction is Timber Frame.

Timber Frame construction, in its modern form has been around since the last century, and during this period, it has had a success rate which is markedly higher than that of conventional block and mortar construction.

In effect, the only difference between Timber Frame and conventional blocks and mortar construction is that the Inner leaf of blockwork is replaced by a Timber Frame structure. Roof, floors, doors, windows, internal finishing and services are the same in both methods of construction, but because the Timber Frame is a dry form of construction, it requires little or no drying-out period.

Why Choose Timber Frame?

Appearance
As the Timber Frame structure is externally clad with block or brickwork and internally finished with plasterboard it means that in appearance the house looks no different to its masonry counterpart.

Energy Efficiency
Unlike Masonry Construction the insulation in a Timber Frame home is contained inside the inner leaf ensuring that no heat is lost in the blockwork. Timber Frame Homes are easy to heat, cosy to live in and can result in savings in heating costs of up to 50%.

Speed of Construction
As all Timber Frame components are manufactured under factory controlled conditions prior to delivery on site, the Timber Frame structural shell can be erected and roofed with felt and tiling battens within days. This allows internal and external trades full access to proceed with their work regardless of the weather. The speed of erection reduces the amount of capital tied up in the work, reduces the interest charges and increases profitability. A house can be fully furnished and ready for occupation in weeks rather than months.

Structural Design
Each house produced by Century Homes is custom built and undergoes an extensive structural analysis. This procedure ensures that the highest standards are maintained both in design and manufacture.

Sound
The sound insulation properties of a Timber Frame Home meet all the requirements of current building regulations.

Durability
All structural timber members are fully protected. As an additional safeguard the external wall timbers are treated with a preservative. The life span of a Timber Frame Home is the same as that of a masonry built home.

Accuracy
With Timber Frame, right angles are true and edges are straight, resulting in greater ease in wallpapering and carpet laying.

Decoration
Timber Frame Homes can be decorated immediately without fear of damp staining or unsightly shrinkage cracks.

Five Bedroom

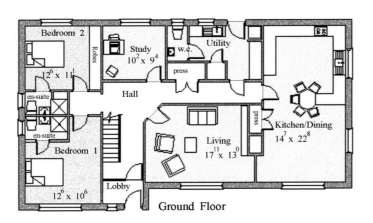

Ground Floor

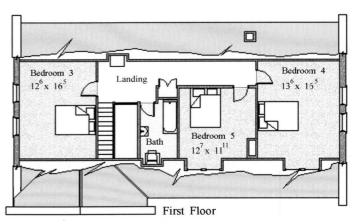

First Floor

Overall Length	54'06"
Overall Width	32'02"
Ground Floor	1469 sq.ft.
First Floor	821 sq.ft.
Floor Area	2290 sq.ft.

This design encorporates a study - an increasingly popular inclusion to many new homes. See page 15 for information on Studies and workspaces.

Construction Costs
For a guideline of costs in Section B see pages 48 and 117.

Additional Options and Services Available. See page 17.

Four Bedroom

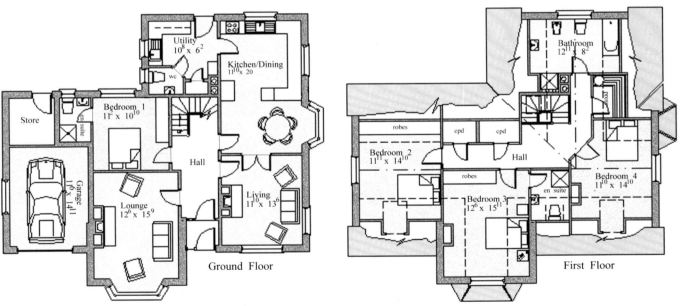

Ground Floor

First Floor

Construction Costs
For a guideline of costs
in Section B see pages
48 and 117.

Minimal use of colour can be very effective - here the
plinth, plaster reveals and barge boards are picked out
in a dark blue.

Overall Length	46'11"
Overall Width	40'08"
Ground Floor	1109 sq.ft.
First Floor	927 sq.ft.
Floor Area	2036 sq.ft.

Additional Options and Services Available. See page 17.

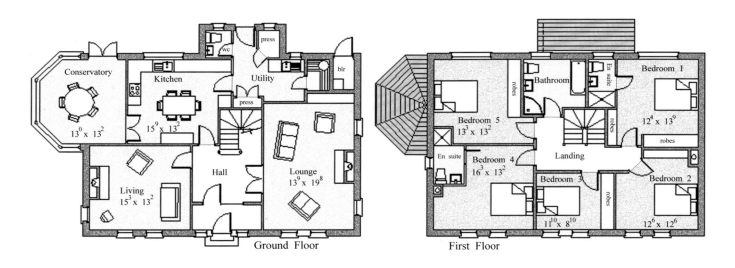

Ground Floor

First Floor

Overall Length	42'02"	
Overall Width	33'02"	
Ground Floor	1209 sq.ft.	
First Floor	1034 sq.ft.	
Floor Area	2243 sq.ft.	

A very simple two storey house. The windows illustrated are all of a uniform shape and stryle and this creates a very bold facade.

Construction Costs
For a guideline of costs in Section B see pages 48 and 117.

Additional Options and Services Available. See page 17.

86

Five Bedroom

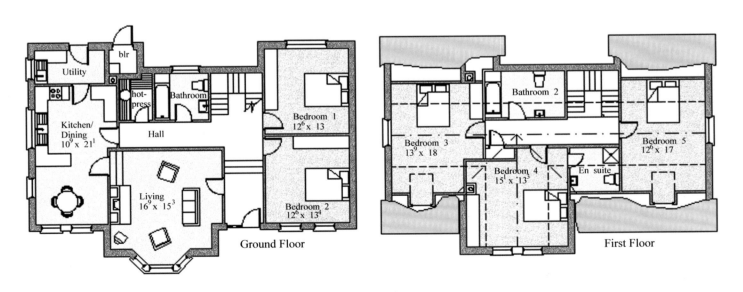

Ground Floor

First Floor

Plan-A-Home
For Construction Cost
Consultants and
Quantity Surveyors.

The creation of a bay window has impact on the appearance
of both the interior and exterior of the house. a bay may
frame an interesting view or provide a niche for sitting
or working in.

Overall Length	48'11"
Overall Width	28'09"
Ground Floor	1255 sq.ft.
First Floor	900 sq.ft.
Floor Area	2155 sq.ft.

Additional Options and Services Available. See page 17.

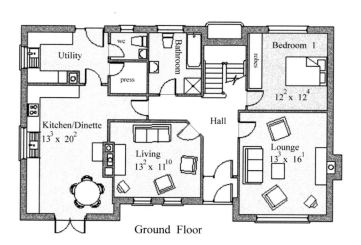

Ground Floor

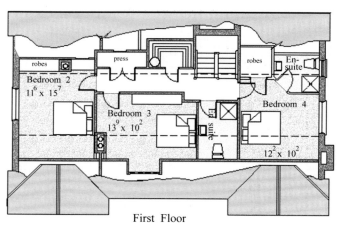

First Floor

Overall Length	47'09"
Overall Width	30'08"
Ground Floor	1250 sq.ft.
First Floor	751 sq.ft.
Floor Area	2001 sq.ft.

Glazing can be an indication of the internal functions of a house. Here a large window indicates the lounge where guests may be entertained. In contrast the more private family room has small twin windows.

Plan-A-Home:
For complete site surveys and analysis.

For a metric/imperial conversion table see page 17.

B 5034

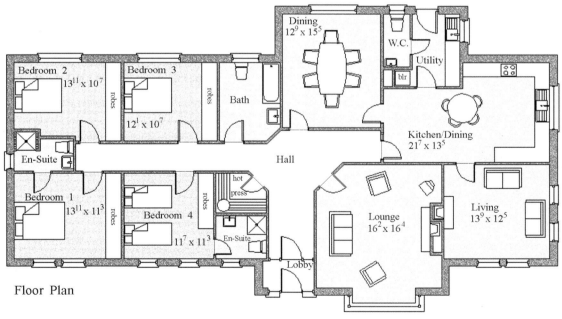

Floor Plan

Dining
12⁹ x 15⁵

W.C.

Utility

blr

Bedroom 2
13¹¹ x 10⁷

robes

Bedroom 3
12¹ x 10⁷

robes

Bath

En-Suite

Hall

Kitchen/Dining
21⁷ x 13⁵

Bedroom 1
13¹¹ x 11³

robes

Bedroom 4
11⁷ x 11³

robes

hot press

En-Suite

Lounge
16² x 16⁴

Living
13⁹ x 12⁵

Lobby

<u>Construction Costs</u>
For a guideline of costs
in Section B see pages
48 and 117.

All of the designs in this book have been created
to illustrate certain forms, layouts, details and
finishes. Plan-A-Home will always tailor a
design specifically to your needs.

Overall Length 71'08"
Overall Width 28'02"
Floor Area 2086 sq.ft.

Additional Options and Services Available. See page 17.

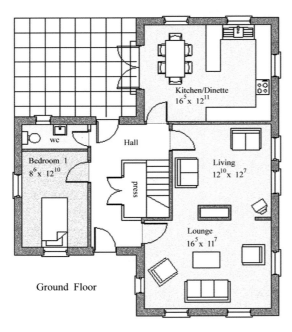

Ground Floor

Kitchen/Dinette
16⁵ x 12¹¹

wc

Hall

Bedroom 1
8⁶ x 12¹⁰

press

Living
12¹⁰ x 12⁷

Lounge
16⁵ x 11⁷

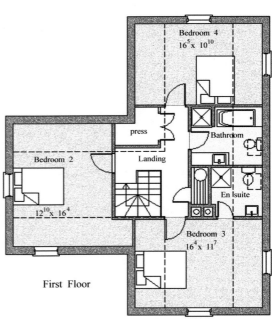

First Floor

Bedroom 4
16⁵ x 10¹⁰

press

Bathroom

Bedroom 2

Landing

En Isuite

12¹⁰ x 16⁴

Bedroom 3
16⁴ x 11⁷

Overall Length	39'08"
Overall Width	34'02"
Ground Floor	874 sq.ft.
First Floor	847 sq.ft.
Floor Area	1721 sq.ft.

A very elegant house with the windows framed by plain plaster bands. Internally the plan offers versatility of layout.

Construction Costs
For a guideline of costs in Section B see pages 48 and 117.

Additional Options and Services Available. See page 17.

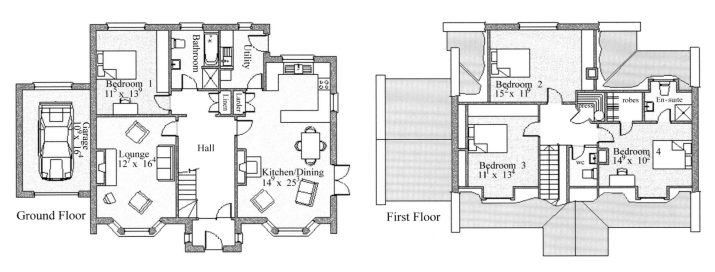

Ground Floor

Bedroom 1
11⁵ x 13⁹

Bathroom

Utility

Garage
10⁹ x 16⁴

Lounge
12⁷ x 16⁴

Hall

Larder

Linen

Kitchen/Dining
14⁹ x 25³

First Floor

Bedroom 2
15² x 11⁹

robes

En-suite

press

Bedroom 3
11¹ x 13⁴

wc

Bedroom 4
14⁹ x 10²

Plan-A-Home
For a full Architectural
Service.

A pretty cottage style dwelling illustrated with
climbing plants framing the traditional entrance
porch. Page 130 has details of this type of
planting.

Overall Length	50'10"
Overall Width	37'01"
Ground Floor	1128 sq.ft.
First Floor	700 sq.ft.
Floor Area	1828 sq.ft.

Additional Options and Services Available. See page 17.

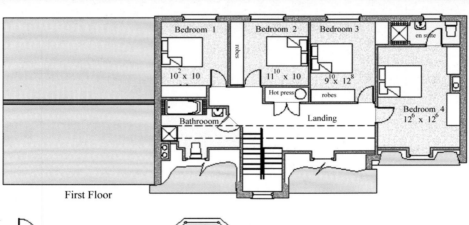

First Floor

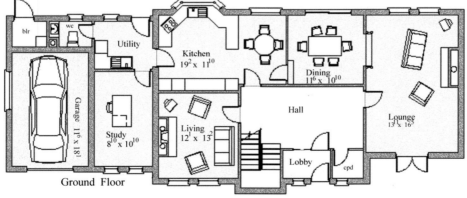

Ground Floor

Overall Length 69'04"
Overall Width 30'06"
Ground Floor 1268 sq.ft.
First Floor 905 sq.ft.
Floor Area 2173 sq.ft.

The stairwell is an interesting feature of this design both internally and externally. Stained glass is a traditional craft undergoing a popular revival. The study and utility are optional and have been shown on the plan but not on the computer image.

Plan-A-Home
For Interior Planning and Design.

Additional Options and Services Available. See page 17.

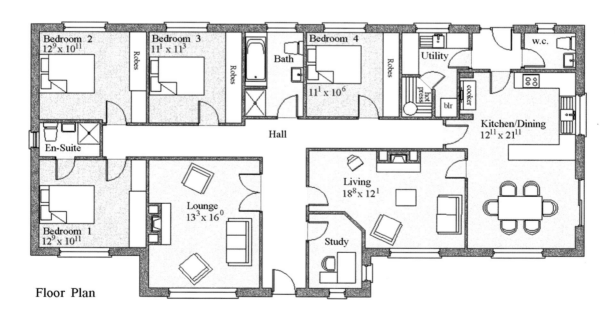

Floor Plan

Bedroom 2
12^9 x 10^{11}

Robes

Bedroom 3
11^1 x 11^3

Robes

Bath

Bedroom 4

11^1 x 10^6

Robes

Utility

w.c.

cooker

blr

hot press

Kitchen/Dining
12^{11} x 21^{11}

En-Suite

Hall

Living
18^8 x 12^1

Lounge
13^3 x 16^0

Bedroom 1
12^9 x 10^{11}

Study

Construction Costs
For a guideline of costs
in Section B see pages
48 and 117.

All plans are flexible and open to change. Use ideas
from the different designs illustrated to discuss
with us what you hope to achieve in your home.

Overall Length 66'04"
Overall Width 28'11"
Floor Area 1860 sq.ft.

Additional Options and Services Available. See page 17.

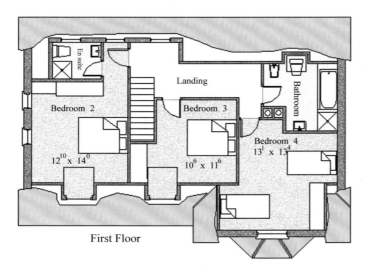

First Floor

En suite

Landing

Bathroom

Bedroom 2

Bedroom 3

Bedroom 4
13^1 x 13^4

12^{10} x 14^0

10^6 x 11^6

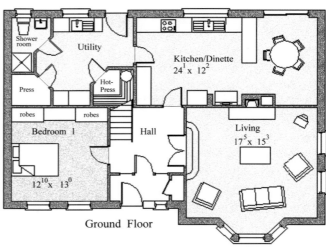

Ground Floor

Shower room

Utility

Press

Hot-Press

robes　robes

Bedroom 1

Kitchen/Dinette
24^1 x 12^2

Hall

Living
17^5 x 15^3

12^{10} x 13^0

Overall Length	42'09"
Overall Width	32'02"
Ground Floor	1089 sq.ft.
First Floor	806 sq.ft.
Floor Area	1895 sq.ft.

This design is modelled on a basic plan which has proved very popular in the past. Its flexibility means many variations in plan and elevation are achieveable.

Construction Costs
For a guideline of costs in Section B see pages 48 and 117.

Additional Options and Services Available. See page 17.

Four Bedroom

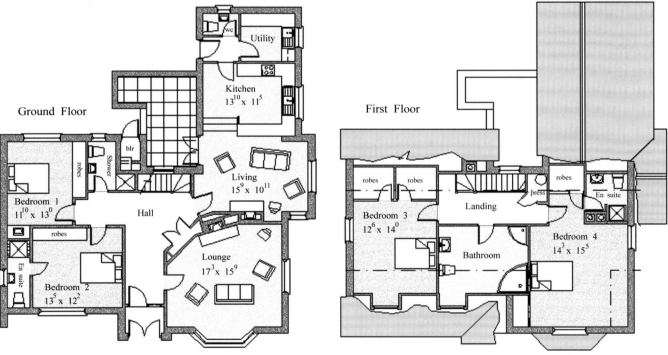

Ground Floor

wc

Utility

Kitchen
13¹⁰ x 11⁵

blr

Shower

robes

Living
15⁹ x 10¹¹

Bedroom 1
11¹⁰ x 13⁰

Hall

robes

En suite

Bedroom 2
13⁵ x 12²

Lounge
17³ x 15⁹

First Floor

robes robes

press

robes

En suite

Bedroom 3
12⁶ x 14⁰

Landing

Bathroom

Bedroom 4
14³ x 15⁵

Plan-A-Home
For Mortgage
Supervision.

This plan exhibits a well laid out ground floor. It is also a good example of flexibility of space. There is plenty of scope to create en-suite showers off all bedrooms.

Overall Length 47'00"
Overall Width 52'06"
Ground Floor 1407 sq.ft.
First Floor 832 sq.ft.
Floor Area 2239 sq.ft.

Additional Options and Services Available. See page 17.

Four Bedroom

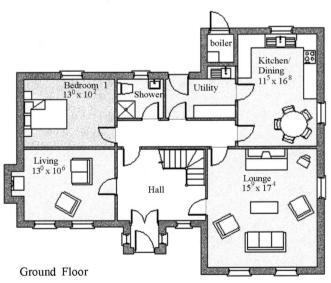

Ground Floor

- boiler
- Kitchen/ Dining 11⁵ x 16⁸
- Utility
- Shower
- Bedroom 1 13⁰ x 10²
- Living 13⁰ x 10⁶
- Hall
- Lounge 15⁹ x 17⁴

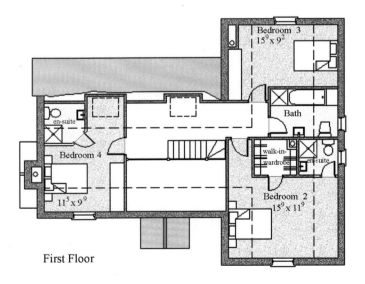

First Floor

- Bedroom 3 15⁹ x 9²
- Bath
- en-suite
- Bedroom 4 11⁵ x 9⁹
- walk-in-wardrobe
- en-suite
- Bedroom 2 15⁹ x 11⁹

Overall Length	44'01"
Overall Width	22'11"
Ground Floor	1119 sq.ft.
First Floor	836 sq.ft.
Floor Area	1955 sq.ft.

The influence of the old school house is very much apparent in this design. The arched doorway and stone finish embellish what is essentially a simple building.

Plan-A-Home
Have offices in Dublin, Donegal, Cork and Galway. See inside back cover.

Additional Options and Services Available. See page 17.

Four Bedroom

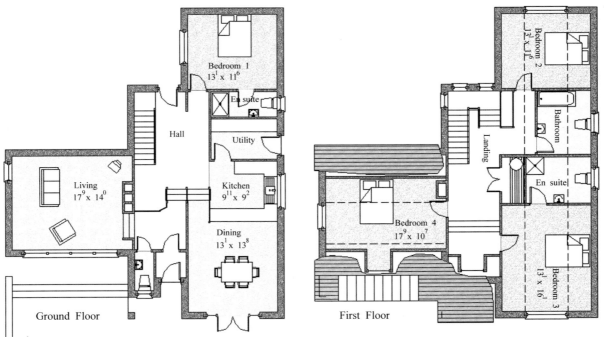

Ground Floor

- Bedroom 1 13' x 11'6"
- En suite
- Hall
- Utility
- Living 17'9" x 14'0"
- Kitchen 9'11" x 9'2"
- Dining 13'1" x 13'8"

First Floor

- Bedroom 2 13'1" x 11'6"
- Bathroom
- Landing
- En suite
- Bedroom 4 17'9" x 10'7"
- Bedroom 3 13'1" x 16'1"

Construction Costs
For a guideline of costs in Section B see pages 48 and 117.

Here is a fine example of one of our newer designs. A spacious and well glazed house that would most be appropriate for a southerly aspect.

Overall Length 41'00"
Overall Width 47'03"
Ground Floor 1078 sq.ft.
First Floor 998 sq.ft.
Floor Area 2076 sq.ft.

Additional Options and Services Available. See page 17.

Four Bedroom

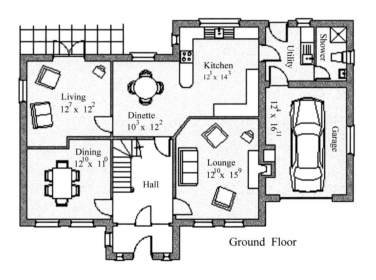

Living 12⁷ x 12²

Kitchen 12¹ x 14³

Utility

Shower

Dinette 10³ x 12²

Dining 12¹⁰ x 11⁰

Hall

Lounge 12¹⁰ x 15⁹

Garage 12⁴ x 16¹¹

Ground Floor

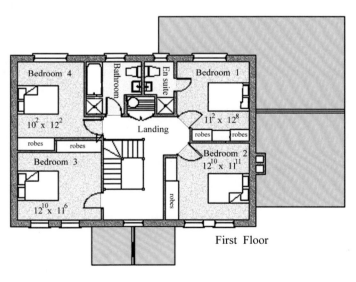

Bedroom 4 10² x 12²

Bathroom

En suite

Bedroom 1 11² x 12⁸

robes   robes

Landing

robes   robes

Bedroom 3 12¹⁰ x 11⁶

Bedroom 2 12¹⁰ x 11¹¹

robes

First Floor

Overall Length	50'10"
Overall Width	37'08"
Ground Floor	1115 sq.ft.
First Floor	837 sq.ft.
Floor Area	1952 sq.ft.

Internally this plan is flexible and would lend itself to open plan. See page 11 for ideas on how to define living spaces.

Construction Costs
For a guideline of costs in Section B see pages 48 and 117.

Additional Options and Services Available. See page 17.

Five Bedroom

B 5044

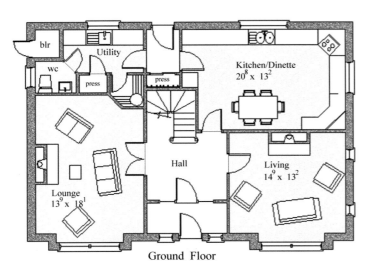

Ground Floor

- blr
- Utility
- wc
- press
- press
- Kitchen/Dinette 20⁸ x 13²
- Hall
- Living 14⁹ x 13²
- Lounge 13⁹ x 18¹

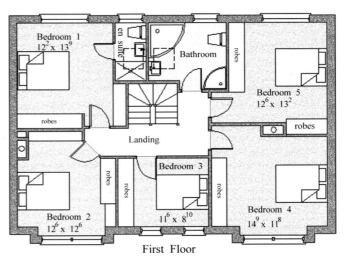

First Floor

- Bedroom 1 12² x 13⁹
- en suite
- Bathroom
- robes
- robes
- Bedroom 5 12⁶ x 13²
- Landing
- robes
- robes
- robes
- Bedroom 3 11⁶ x 8¹⁰
- robes
- Bedroom 2 12⁶ x 12⁶
- Bedroom 4 14⁹ x 11⁸

<u>Plan-A-Home</u>
For advice on Planning

The external appearance of a house can vary dramatically depending on the material used. The architect will advise you on the suitability of different material finishes for your particular site location.

Overall Length	41'04"
Overall Width	29'07"
Ground Floor	1065 sq.ft.
First Floor	1032 sq.ft.
Floor Area	2097 sq.ft.

Additional Options and Services Available. See page 17.

Four Bedroom

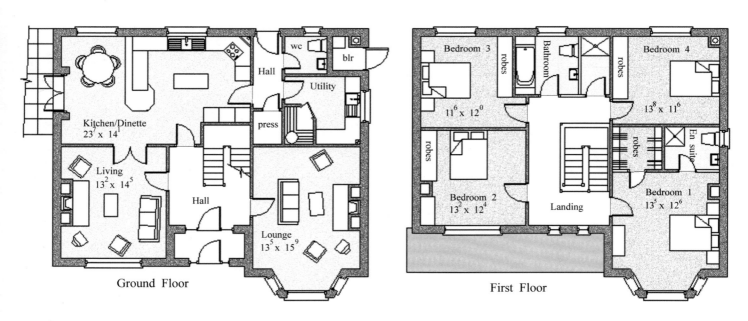

Ground Floor

Kitchen/Dinette
23^7 x 14^1

Living
13^2 x 14^5

Hall

wc

blr

Hall

Utility

press

Lounge
13^5 x 15^9

First Floor

Bedroom 3
11^6 x 12^0

robes

Bathroom

robes

Bedroom 4
13^8 x 11^6

robes

robes

En suite

Bedroom 2
13^2 x 12^4

Landing

Bedroom 1
13^5 x 12^6

Overall Length	39'04"
Overall Width	35'02"
Ground Floor	965 sq.ft.
First Floor	1118 sq.ft.
Floor Area	2083 sq.ft.

The double height bay is an attractive feature of this design. It is noteworthy that this house has a back porch independent of both utility room and kitchen. See planning interiors on page 12 for information.

<u>Plan-A-Home</u>
For a complete Architectural Service.

Additional Options and Services Available. See page 17.

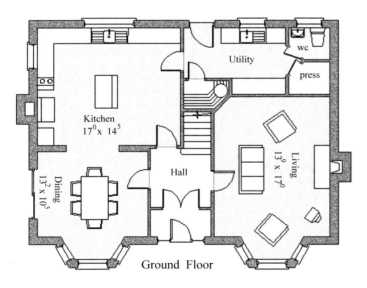

Kitchen
17^0 x 14^5

Utility

wc

press

Dining
13^2 x 10^5

Hall

Living
13^9 x 17^0

Ground Floor

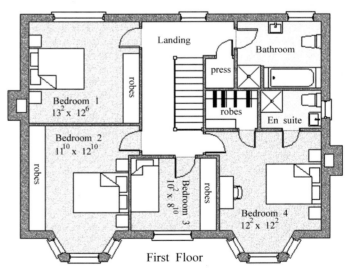

Landing

Bathroom

press

Bedroom 1
13^2 x 12^6

robes

robes

En suite

Bedroom 2
11^{10} x 12^{10}

robes

Bedroom 3
10^2 x 8^{10}

robes

Bedroom 4
12^2 x 12^2

First Floor

Construction Costs
For a guideline of costs
in Section B see pages
48 and 117.

Handsome full height bays and attention to detail
in the glazing around the doorway affords this house
an elegant and balanced facade.

Overall Length	36'09"
Overall Width	30'02"
Ground Floor	921 sq.ft.
First Floor	894 sq.ft.
Floor Area	1815 sq.ft.

For a metric/imperial conversion table see page 17.

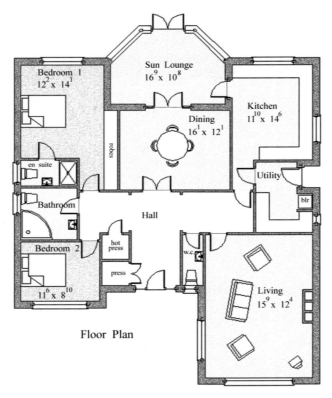

Floor Plan

Overall Length 44'08"
Overall Width 54'01"
Floor Area 1716 sq.ft.

The sun lounge is an unusual feature of this design.
On entering the house a view is afforded right
through the dining room and sun lounge.

Construction Costs
For a guideline of costs
in Section B see pages
48 and 117.

Additional Options and Services Available. See page 17.

Five Bedroom

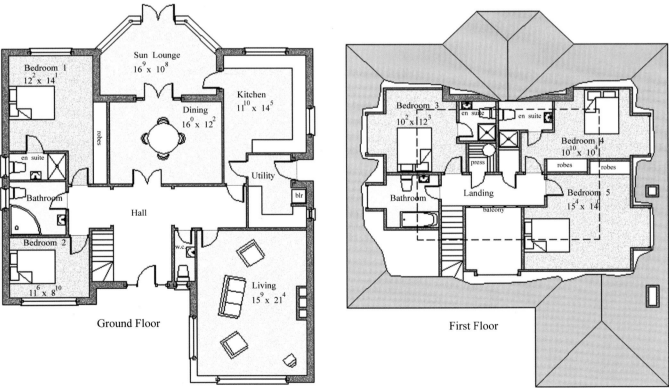

Ground Floor

- Bedroom 1 12^2 x 14^1
- Sun Lounge 16^9 x 10^8
- Kitchen 11^{10} x 14^5
- Dining 16^0 x 12^2
- robes
- en suite
- Bathroom
- Utility
- blr
- Hall
- Bedroom 2 11^6 x 8^{10}
- w.c.
- Living 15^9 x 21^4

First Floor

- Bedroom 3 10^2 x 11^3
- en suite
- en suite
- Bedroom 4 10^{10} x 10^1
- press
- robes   robes
- Bathroom
- Landing
- Bedroom 5 15^4 x 14^1
- balcony

Plan-A-Home
For Commercial as well
as Domestic Architecture.

Based on design 5047, this house has a similar
ground floor plan and has been extended into
the roofspace to provide further bedrooms.

Overall Length	44'08"
Overall Width	54'00"
Ground Floor	1716 sq.ft.
First Floor	796 sq.ft.
Floor Area	2512 sq.ft.

Additional Options and Services Available. See page 17.

Three Bedroom

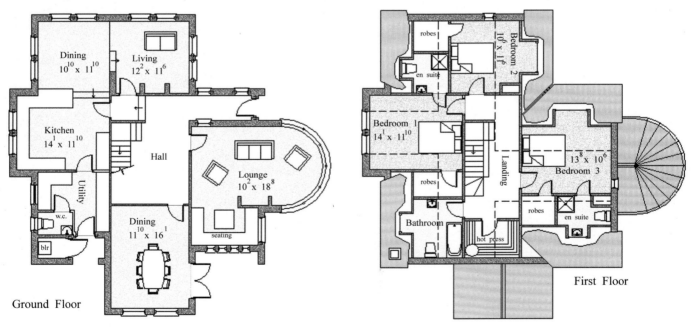

Dining
10^{10} x 11^{10}

Living
12^2 x 11^6

Kitchen
14^1 x 11^{10}

Hall

Utility

w.c.

blr

Lounge
10^2 x 18^8

seating

Dining
11^{10} x 16^1

Ground Floor

robes

en suite

Bedroom 2
10^6 x 1^6

Bedroom 1
14^1 x 11^{10}

robes

Landing

Bathroom

hot press

robes

13^8 x 10^6
Bedroom 3

en suite

First Floor

Overall Length 47'03"
Overall Width   48'06"
Floor Area   1312 sq.ft.
First Floor   906 sq.ft.
Floor Area   2218 sq.ft.

Our front cover illustration - viewed another angle.
This design, a marriage of old and new, combines many
interesting features: circular bay, double height entrance
and winter and summer spaces.

Plan-A-Home
Have an in-house
Computer Graphics
Bureau.

Additional Options and Services Available. See page 17.

Four Bedroom

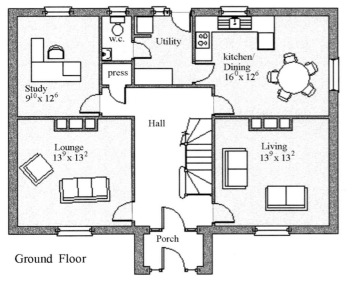

Ground Floor

w.c.

Utility

press

kitchen/
Dining
16^0x 12^6

Study
9^{10}x 12^6

Hall

Lounge
13^9x 13^2

Living
13^9x 13^2

Porch

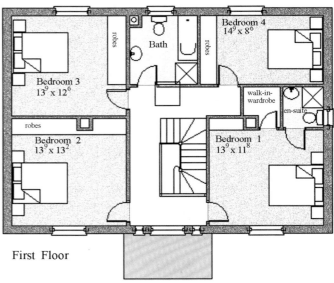

First Floor

robes

Bath

robes

Bedroom 4
14^9x 8^6

Bedroom 3
13^9x 12^6

walk-in-
wardrobe

en-suite

robes

Bedroom 2
13^9x 13^2

Bedroom 1
13^9x 11^8

<u>Construction Costs</u>
For a guideline of costs
in Section B see pages
48 and 117.

The influence of the past can be seen in the clean form
and simply structured layout of this design.

Overall Length	39'04"
Overall Width	32'11"
Ground Floor	1005 sq.ft.
First Floor	918 sq.ft.
Floor Area	1923 sq.ft.

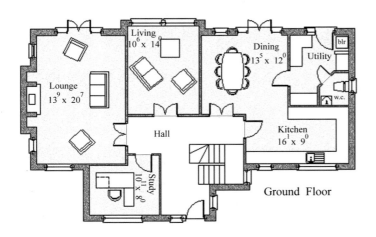

Living 10⁶ x 14⁰

Dining 13⁵ x 12⁰

Utility

blr

Lounge 13⁹ x 20⁷

w.c.

Hall

Kitchen 16¹ x 9⁰

Study 10¹¹ x 8⁰

Ground Floor

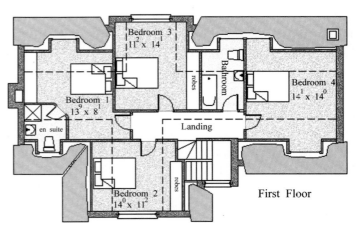

Bedroom 3 11² x 14¹

Bathroom

robes

Bedroom 4 14¹ x 14⁰

Bedroom 1 13⁹ x 8¹

en suite

Landing

Bedroom 2 14⁰ x 11²

robes

First Floor

Overall Length	50'06"
Overall Width	32'04"
Ground Floor	1193 sq.ft.
First Floor	931 sq.ft.
Floor Area	2124 sq.ft.

A 50 degree roof pitch affords extra floor area within the roofspace of this dwelling. Internal features such as the inglenook fireplace and dog leg stair provide points of focus within rooms.

Construction Costs
For a guideline of costs in Section B see pages 48 and 117.

For a metric/imperial conversion table see page 17.

Four Bedroom

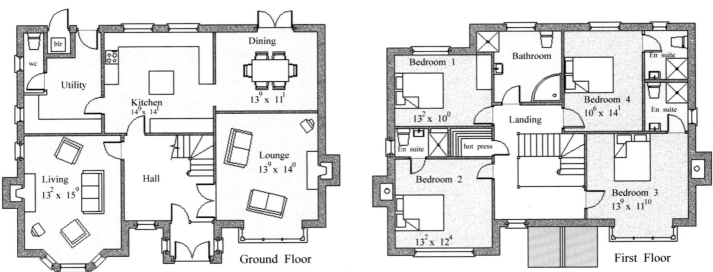

Ground Floor

First Floor

Plan-A-Home
Provide a Landscape
Design Service.

This plan sports a large upstairs bathroom. Pages 14 and 22 contain information on planning a luxury bathroom.

Overall Length	41'08"
Overall Width	34'01"
Ground Floor	1153 sq.ft.
First Floor	1008 sq.ft.
Floor Area	2161 sq.ft.

Additional Options and Services Available. See page 17.

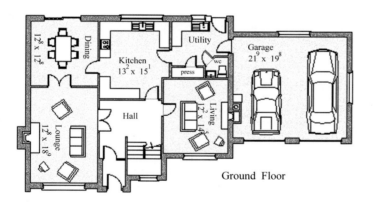

Dining 12'⁸ x 12'⁸

Kitchen 13'² x 15'¹

Utility

wc

press

Garage 21'⁹ x 19'⁸

Hall

Living 12'² x 14'⁶

Lounge 12'⁸ x 18'⁰

Ground Floor

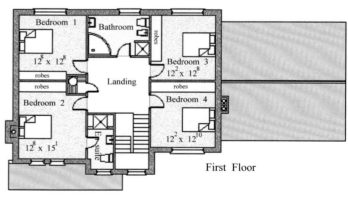

Bedroom 1

Bathroom

robes

12'⁸ x 12'⁸

robes

robes

Landing

Bedroom 3 12'² x 12'⁸

robes

Bedroom 2

Ensuite

Bedroom 4

12'⁸ x 15'¹

12'² x 12'¹⁰

First Floor

Overall Length	61'04"
Overall Width	34'03"
Ground Floor	1092 sq.ft.
First Floor	961 sq.ft.
Floor Area	2053 sq.ft.

The utility room needs to be planned to accommodate all your needs. Here the utility has back door and garage access. See page 14 for information on utility rooms.

<u>Plan-A-Home</u>
Have offices in Dublin, Galway, Cork and Donegal. See inside back pages.

Additional Options and Services Available. See page 17.

108

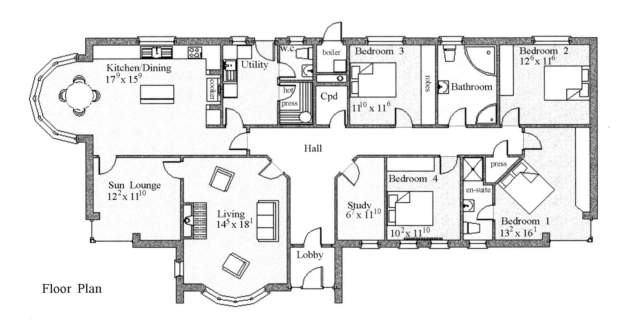

Kitchen/Dining
17⁹ x 15⁹

Utility

w.c.

boiler

Bedroom 3

Bedroom 2
12⁶ x 11⁶

cooker

hot press

Cpd

robes

Bathroom

11¹⁰ x 11⁶

Hall

press

Sun Lounge
12² x 11¹⁰

Living
14⁵ x 18¹

Bedroom 4

en-suite

Study
6⁷ x 11¹⁰

10² x 11¹⁰

Bedroom 1
13² x 16¹

Lobby

Floor Plan

<u>Construction Costs</u>
For a guideline of costs in Section B see pages 48 and 117.

Within this design the dinette is formed in a semi-circular annex off the kitchen. For details on planning for island units, ranges and dining areas see Page 13.

Overall Length 78'08"
Overall Width 37'08"
Floor Area 2122 sq.ft.

Additional Options and Services Available. See page 17.

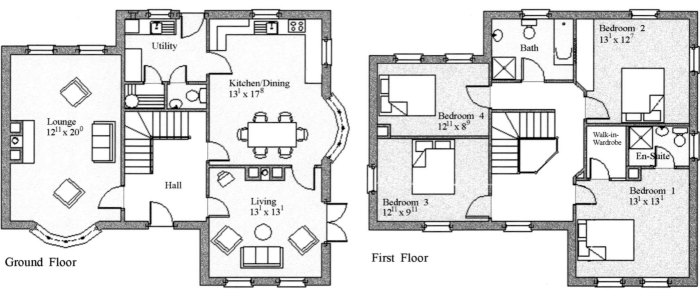

Ground Floor

First Floor

Overall Length	38'03"
Overall Width	33'02"
Ground Floor	934 sq.ft.
First Floor	850 sq.ft.
Floor Area	1784 sq.ft.

A canopy porch, varying window types and decorative quoins and bands to the plasterwork are several of the notable elements which work together to form the facade of this dwelling.

Construction Costs
For a guideline of costs in Section B see pages 48 and 117.

Four Bedroom

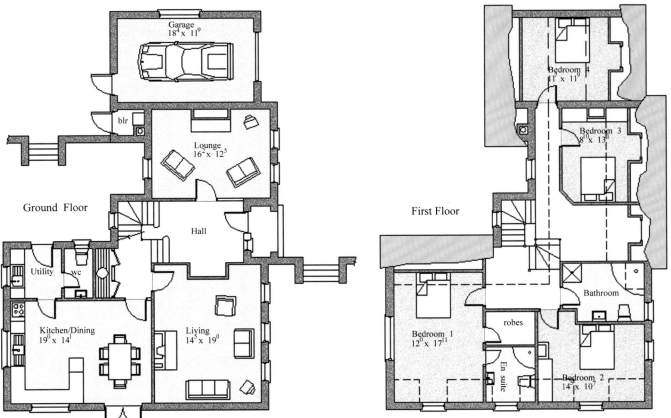

Ground Floor

Garage
18⁴ x 11⁹

blr

Lounge
16² x 12⁵

Hall

Utility   wc

Kitchen/Dining
19⁰ x 14¹

Living
14⁵ x 19⁰

First Floor

Bedroom 4
11' x 11⁹

Bedroom 3
8¹⁰ x 13¹¹

Bathroom

robes

Bedroom 1
12⁰ x 17¹¹

En suite

Bedroom 2
14¹ x 10⁷

Plan-A-Home
For fully computer
generated Plans and
Elevations.

An interesting 'L' shaped split level layout with the
main entrance at one side. The main entrance to your
home should be designed to accommodate your needs
and access to the site.

Overall Length 35'09"
Overall Width 55'05"
Ground Floor 1029 sq.ft.
First Floor 1082 sq.ft.
Floor Area 2328 sq.ft.

Additional Options and Services Available. See page 17.

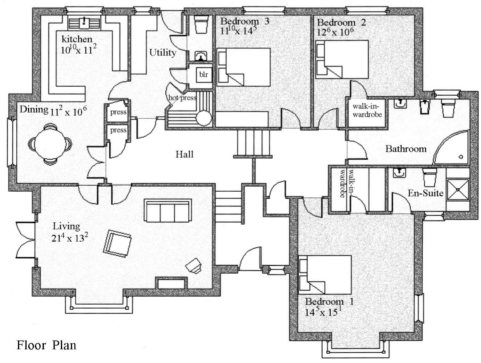

Floor Plan

Overall Length 58'00"
Overall Width   44'09"
Floor Area   1814 sq.ft.

There are velux windows high in the roof of this design which provide light to the internal hallways. Refer to page 11 for information on creating interesting circulation spaces.

Plan-A-Home
For Comprehensive
Specification
Documents.

Additional Options and Services Available. See page 17.

112

Living
14¹ x 13⁵

Kitchen/Dinette
22¹⁰ x 11²

Hall

hot press

press

Utility

w.c.

Lounge
16¹ x 16⁵

Garage 19⁹ x 17⁷

Ground Floor

Bedroom 1
14¹ x 9¹⁰

Landing

Bedrooom 4
9⁶ x 10²

Bedrooom 5
13⁰ x 18¹⁰

robes

en suite

robes

en suite

Bedroom 2
14¹ x 9¹⁰

Bathroom

Bedrooom 3
19⁸ x 15³

First Floor

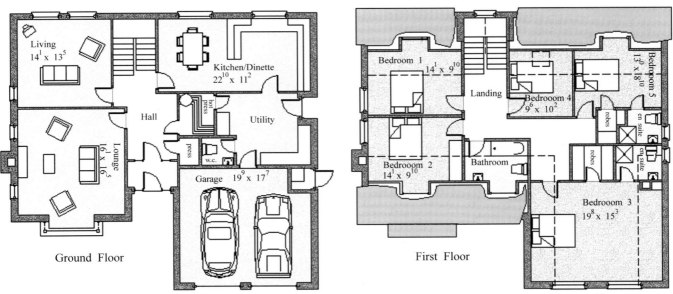

Construction Costs
For a guideline of costs in Section B see pages 48 and 117.

Brick is a very versatile medium and is available in many different colours. Coloured mortar and roof tiles can be used to compliment or contrast with the chosen brick.

Overall Length 45'11"
Overall Width   42'08"
Ground Floor   1147 sq.ft.
First Floor   1190 sq.ft.
Floor Area   2337 sq.ft.

Additional Options and Services Available. See page 17.

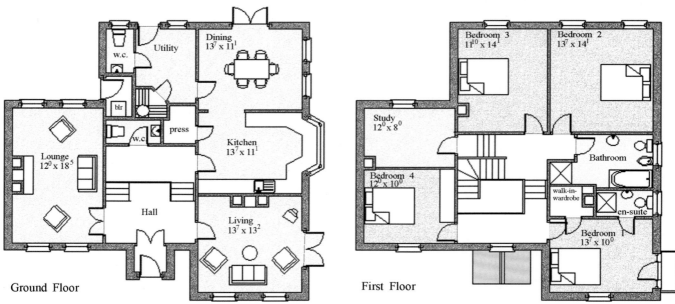

Ground Floor

First Floor

Overall Length 42'00"
Overall Width   37'08"
Ground Floor   1100 sq.ft.
First Floor   1070 sq.ft.
Floor Area   2170 sq.ft.

Split level arises out of the need or desire to have
the house on more than one level. It may be dictated
to by a slope or step in your actual site.

<u>Construction Costs</u>
For a guideline of costs
in Section B see pages
48 and 117.

Additional Options and Services Available. See page 17.

Floor Plan

Bedroom 1 13^1 x 11^9

Bedroom 2 14^1 x 11^9

Bedroom 3 10^2 x 11^9

Bedroom 4 13^1 x 10^9

en-suite

steps

press

hot press

Bath

Kitchen 14^0 x 10^9

blr

press

Utility

W.C.

Garage

Conservatory 11^8 x 12^7

Lounge 15^5 x 17^8

Reception

Living 15^5 x 14^1

Dining 10^9 x 11^3

steps

<u>Plan-A-Home</u>
For Computer Generated
3-Dimensional
Architectural Models.

This well organised layout changes in level to define space. The more public living rooms are located at the front of the house with the private bedroom wing at the rear.

Overall Length 78'00"
Overall Width 29'06"
Floor Area 2313 sq.ft.

Additional Options and Services Available. See page 17.

Planting Solutions

Suppliers of Planting by Numbers garden templates/patterns

LET US SOLVE YOUR PLANTING PROBLEMS

The finished product from
Planting Solutions

FULL RANGE OF SERVICES

Consultancy

Site visits

Outline plans

Perspective drawings

Planting maps

Budget estimates

D.I.Y. PACKS
We can source and
supply everything you
will need.

CONTRACT
Free estimates from
your drawings

D.I.Y.Template

FREE COLOUR BROCHURE

Contact <u>Planting Solutions</u>

Derra, Kilkishen, Co. Clare, Rep. of Ireland.

Tel: 061 367283 Fax: 061 367094 e-mail: info@ps.iol.ie

Guideline Specifications
Section B

Stage A

Roof: Tegral 2000 Slates.
External Walls: smooth render.
Fascia/soffit: upvc or aluminium.
Windows/external doors: upvc double glazed.
Internal doors: Hardwood panel.
Architrave/skirting: Hardwood.

Stage B

All as detailed on page 48 including for:
Hardwood kitchen/utility units;
2400mm high wall tiling to baths, showers &
W.C.'s including 500mm tiling above
worktops.
Decoration to all external/internal walls,
ceilings and second fix joinery only.

Stage C

Siteworks as detailed with gravel drive & kerbs.

plan	stage	region 1	region 2	region 3
5029	A	115,823	129,722	143,991
	B	146,938	164,570	182,673
	C	160,516	179,778	199,553
5030	A	113,014	126,575	140,499
	B	142,581	159,691	177,257
	C	156,057	174,784	194,010
5031	A	126,156	141,295	156,837
	B	153,919	172,390	191,352
	C	167,395	187,482	208,105
5032	A	111,982	125,420	139,217
	B	138,678	155,319	172,404
	C	152,153	170,412	189,157
5033	A	98,766	110,618	122,785
	B	127,898	143,246	159,003
	C	141,374	158,339	175,756
5034	A	118,145	132,322	146,877
	B	147,517	165,219	183,393
	C	160,993	180,312	200,146
5035	A	84,105	94,198	104,559
	B	108,495	121,514	134,881
	C	121,970	136,607	151,633
5036	A	110,892	121,982	135,400
	B	135,368	148,905	165,285
	C	148,844	163,729	181,739
5037	A	138,045	154,611	171,618
	B	165,252	185,082	205,441
	C	178,483	199,901	221,890
5038	A	106,051	118,778	131,843
	B	130,323	145,961	162,017
	C	143,816	161,074	178,792
5039	A	97,507	109,208	121,221
	B	122,874	137,619	152,758
	C	136,350	152,712	169,510
5040	A	120,447	134,901	149,740
	B	152,690	171,013	189,825
	C	166,166	186,106	206,578

Please Note: The prices listed here are for guideline purposes only and are indicative of contract values in €uro's current at Spring 2003.

plan	stage	region 1	region 2	region 3
5041	A	103,820	116,279	129,069
	B	133,946	150,020	166,522
	C	147,422	165,113	183,275
5042	A	126,712	141,917	157,528
	B	151,511	169,693	188,359
	C	167,715	187,841	208,504
5043	A	115,359	129,202	143,414
	B	142,695	159,819	177,399
	C	156,206	174,951	194,195
5044	A	105,355	117,998	130,977
	B	133,469	149,486	165,929
	C	146,945	164,579	182,682
5045	A	108,562	121,589	134,964
	B	137,706	154,231	171,197
	C	151,182	169,324	187,950
5046	A	99,164	111,063	123,280
	B	122,304	136,980	152,048
	C	135,780	152,073	168,801
5047	A	107,522	120,424	133,671
	B	131,630	147,426	163,643
	C	145,106	162,519	180,396
5048	A	140,925	157,836	175,198
	B	177,215	198,480	220,313
	C	190,690	213,573	237,066
5049	A	140,340	157,181	174,470
	B	171,145	191,682	212,767
	C	184,620	206,775	229,520
5050	A	102,172	114,432	127,020
	B	124,593	139,545	154,895
	C	138,069	154,637	171,648
5051	A	121,962	136,597	151,623
	B	147,706	165,431	183,628
	C	161,182	180,523	200,381
5052	A	115,862	129,766	144,040
	B	150,145	168,162	186,660
	C	163,620	183,255	203,413
5053	A	130,797	146,492	162,606
	B	160,683	179,965	199,761
	C	174,158	195,057	216,514
5054	A	126,194	138,813	154,083
	B	148,765	163,642	181,642
	C	162,241	178,465	198,096
5055	A	106,436	117,080	128,788
	B	129,771	142,748	157,023
	C	143,247	157,571	173,329
5056	A	140,852	157,754	175,107
	B	167,440	187,533	208,162
	C	180,916	202,626	224,915
5057	A	112,262	125,733	139,564
	B	137,052	153,499	170,384
	C	153,223	171,610	190,487
5058	A	136,739	153,148	169,994
	B	166,623	186,617	207,145
	C	180,098	201,710	223,898
5059	A	117,954	132,109	146,641
	B	145,501	162,961	180,887
	C	158,977	178,054	197,640
5060	A	133,148	149,126	165,529
	B	163,923	183,593	203,789
	C	176,787	198,002	219,782

Landscape

Ireland from its rocky mountain tops to wild bog, from lush lowlands to the ever pervading ocean; this small island has one of the most magnificently varied and dramatic landscapes of anywhere in the world. The new homebuilder carries with them a responsibility not only to construct a building that can meet their own needs but also one which blends with the existing landscape in a sensitive manner. All of the County Planning offices in Ireland have guidelines on new development in their areas, your architect will be able to advise you on this or you can obtain information direct from the respective Planning Office. These guidelines are designed in conjunction with the area plan to aid new development and to protect and preserve the existing landscape. It is advisable to consult your county planning office before purchasing a site to ensure that it is indeed suitable for development.

No two sites are the same and each must be analysed by the architect in advance of a sketch design being prepared. Part of this analysis will involve a measured survey including recording the dimensions of the site, levels and any existing structures or substantial landmarks. If you are buying a site this type of survey may need to be undertaken for land registry. The following section is designed to make you aware of some of the issues which may have a bearing on how the site can have a direct bearing on the development of the design of your house and also the importance of having a building which is tailored specifically to its site.

The Site

There has been a trend in this country over the last few years to completely clear sites where building is to be carried out. The widescale clearance is not necessary to aid the building process and is also detrimental to the character of the site. Very often the very features which made the site attractive in the first place are wiped out. It is important to be aware of the importance of preserving existing features of a site. Where possible all mature planting including trees and hedgerows should be maintained. These can be of great benefit to the dwelling not only from the point of shelter but also to enhance the look of the new building and to help it to blend into the site. If you look at some of the older traditional houses you will notice how great care was taken to locate the building within its site, be it nestled on a hillside or standing by the road. Many of the rules which governed the siting of these older houses still apply today.

Aspect

It is important to avail of natural light and therefore to take full advantage of the daily path of the sun. The sun rises in the East so therefore it is appropriate that morning rooms such as bedrooms and kitchens avail of this orientation. Westerly facing rooms will receive evening light. South facing rooms have the best aspect having sunlight from mid-day through to evening. Your architect will discuss this with you and help you to prioritise room layout.

View

It is most likely that you will have chosen your site more for its view than for any other single point. It is important to discuss which views you would wish to avail of from which rooms with the architect. The architect will ensure that a balance is struck in order to maximise view and to maintain a satisfactory level of light. For example if the best view from your site is north facing it will be important to try to bring light into the building from another direction.

Access

It is important that your site can be reached by road. If you have to create a new access or do extensive works to make an existing laneway passable this could add greatly to you overall building cost. There may also be other restrictions to accessing public roads and any entrance must comply with safety regulations as set down by the Roads Engineer.

Size and Servicing

It is, of course, important that your site is large enough to accommodate the type of house you want to have but it is also important at this stage to be aware of the possibilities, should your needs change and you wish to extend in the future. The size of your site may also be important depending on whether or not the site is serviced by Mains drainage. If not, you may have to use an alternative means of waste disposal, these need to be a specific distance away from both the new and any existing dwellings. The Health Officer will advise you on whether or not the site is suitable for a septic tank or what other options are open to you. The electric and water authorities will also be able to advise you also on their respective service in relation to your site.

Boundaries

There are many reasons for denoting the boundary of property be it in built or planted form. A wall, hedge or fence can be desirable for many reasons as shelter for house and garden, as an enclosure for children and pets, for security or for purely aesthetic reasons. Where possible existing walls and hedging should be maintained. Again it is important to consider the traditional elements used in your area when deciding on walls, gates and fences for your property. You should also be aware that structures such as these may be affected by planning constraints and should be discussed in advance with the architect.

Hard Landscaping

The term hard landscaping can refer to all areas which have a hard finish, be it paved or patio areas, paths or retaining walls. You will find that areas such as these can very much be dictated by the siting and layout of your house and in fact it is wise to think of the garden as an extension of the rooms

inside you house and form connections with outside spaces. The location of the patio may be dictated by your desire to have it close to the kitchen or diningroom where it would be practical to have a seating area for eating in fine weather. If you have a large garden you may wish to take advantage of this and have pathways leading away from the house to a patio or barbecue area which can become a type of outside room. Hard landscaping needs careful planning. You should seek advice from your architect on the construction of larger structures such as retaining walls, water features and on technical aspects. Drainage and external lighting are important factors which can require specification documentation. Technical drawings may need to be prepared to illustrate these items. It may be convenient for your builder to do structural landscaping works in conjunction with the construction of your house.

Soft Landscaping

This usually refers to features which are formed from earth and planting. It is this type of landscaping which softens the impact of man made structures and helps merge buildings and garden into the natural surroundings. Planting can be formal denoting boundaries or pathways or random to reflect wild landscape. It can be used in the same way that walls are within a building to define spaces. Existing indigenous plants on your site, such as blackthorn can be trimmed and tamed to form part of a new planting scheme.

They will provide valuable shelter for newly planted saplings and shrubs. The planting of native species is to be encouraged.

It should be noted that shrubbery is often easier to maintain than large grassed areas and in particular where the site is sloping.

Guide to Soft Landscaping for Gardens

The following section attempts to deal with some of the issues that are raised when considering laying out a garden.

Where should I start ?
When and what should I plant ?
How much will it cost ?
Can I tackle the work myself ?

Landscaping will complement any property and make it much more desirable to a potential buyer than a site that is undeveloped. In terms of investment, Landscaping will add value to your property and does not necessarily need to be vastly expensive. Simple, well laid out grassed areas and well positioned hedging will add appeal to the interested buyer.

Houses are built within certain styles. In the garden you have style options too. This may be partially governed by the space you have available and also by the scale and look of your house. A large garden may have room for several themes, whereas a small garden might revolve around a special feature.

It is important to have some idea of your requirements before you start to plan.

The pictures in this page are examples of sometypes of gardens and may assist you in your selection. PLAN-A-HOME can provide a suggested landscape plan to help you along. (Similar to diagram on Pg131).

Your garden should be carefully devised to suit your requirements both in terms of space for planting, recreation and parking. Existing planting on a site can be adapted to form part of the new garden. It is important not to overspend on new planting if you intend selling the house soon after building it.

Formal

Informal

Modern

Traditional

Work in progress (wooden deck)

Work completed

I've bought a site

Congratulations! You probably have a house in mind. Have you a garden in mind also?

The garden can be at the end of a long list of priorities, too often by the time the house is finished the budget for the garden can be used up.

Here, are some suggestions which may help you use your budget wisely.

Plan your garden early.
This will ensure, if you have earthworks to carry out, that all material will be located at convenient places for final spreading thus saving you money.

Start a weed-killing program as soon as possible.
To get topsoil really weed free it may need two or more applications so the sooner you start the better. A weedkiller application prior to soil excavations.

Do not handle or stockpile topsoil in wet weather.
This breaks down the drainage particles in the soil and can take several years to rectify.

Storing and stockpiling topsoil.
Do not stockpile topsoil too high as again this can cause deterioration in the quality of your soil. Topsoil contains living organisms and these live in the top layer of the ground where they have access to light and air.

Plant shelter belts and hedges as soon as possible.
Planting early can save you money, you can choose smaller plants which will be growing as the house is being built (see page 128).

Summary:
Consider the garden as part of the overall design.
Be careful when handling topsoil.
Spray with weedkiller.
Plant the boundaries of the site as soon as possible

How to start a landscape project

There are many considerations to take on board when embarking on and planning a soft landscaping project whether you employ a contractor or carry out the work yourself.

Planning Stage

It is advisable to begin by acquiring some broad information. This can be obtained from the gardening department of your local library of bookstore. It maybe useful to make photocopies of images that appeal to you to help in discussions about the effect you are trying to achieve. It is important that you have a good idea of what you require before you approach any professional. Having formed an opinion on the type of landscaping that you would wish to implement in your garden, it is then time to seek advice from one of the following people.

Landscape Architect
Landscape Designer/Contractor
Garden Centre/Nursery
Horticultural Adviser

Normally, landscape designs are available in two forms, an outline plan and a detailed planting plan as per illustration.

An indication of hard landscaping is often shown on the site layout maps prepared by the architect for planning purposes. This is a good, basic outline to start working out how the hard and soft areas will work together. A further plan covering details of hard surfaces and structural landscape work may be needed. (See landscape section Pg 121).

It is never too early to have your adviser assess the site. From a practical point of view the initial visit should take place when the shell of the house has been completed. Be satisfied with the credentials of your consultant. It is always advisable to ask them if you can see some of their work which they have completed.

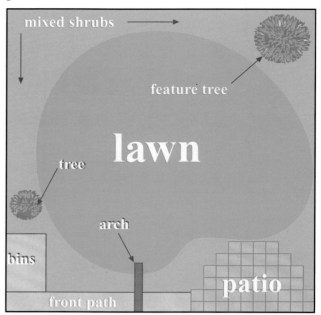

Outline plan

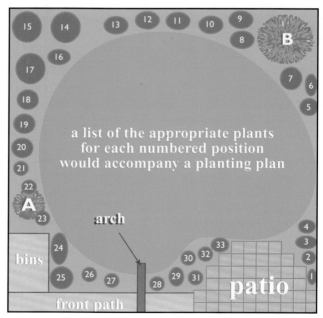

Detail plan

Water lodging

Hard Surface construction

Lawns completed

Feature plants in shrubs

Start work

Having completed the planning stage of the development you now need to consider who will do the work, how much it will cost (see costings guide Pg131) and prioritise your requirements.

Suggested priority check-list

Outline plan
An outline plan is sufficient to get started. It is also a suitable document for seeking prices from contractors.

Drainage
If drainage is necessary, do it first. Try to complete the work under dry conditions.

Hard surfaces/Walls/Fences
These are usually completed next.

Clearing/Grading
Although this work is often completed prior to hard surface landscaping, it is an advantage to carry it out after such work, as surfaces are often damaged during construction work.

Topsoiling
This is normally completed immediately after clearing and grading. If possible, lay your lawns immediately after spreading your topsoil.

Shelterbelt/Hedges
Provided your boundary levels are correct, the sooner you plant the better. Do consider doing some planting before you start building.

Lawns
These are laid last from March to September. For smaller areas, consider using roll out sodding.

Feature Plants
These are normally trees, conifers or shrubs with a distinctive shape and are used to create the overall character of your garden.

Infill plants
These can be annuals, heathers, shrubs, etc. and because they establish themselves quickly, they can be planted last.

Summary:
Follow a natural sequence of events and avoid double work.
Do not spread topsoil until you are ready to lay your lawn.
Avoid laying tarmacadam or finished surfaces until lawns are completed.

Who will I get to do the work?

The Professional Approach

A professional landscape contractor will usually have experience in all types of landscaping. If you decide to go this route, it is a good idea to see some of the work that the contractor has produced. Often, they will have a portfolio of images that reflect the different types of jobs that they have been involved in or it may be possible to talk to their customers. A professional contractor will encourage you to do this. Some time spent on this type of investigative research could save you a lot of frustration during the job. A reliable landscape contractor can be recommended in your area by your local association of landscape contractors.

Tackling the job yourself

If you have built the house yourself you may feel confident enough to deal with any subcontractors that may be needed to complete the heavier or more ambitious tasks attached to landscaping and to cover the rest of the work yourself. Straightforward lawn laying and planting are within the capabilities of anyone with a strong back and a willingness to learn.

Landscape Templates

Professional advise on a sheet couldnít be simpler! Basically the templates are full size plans/patterns of your garden or part of your garden which are printed on sheet material (normally weedsheet fabric or paper). You lay the plan over the area of your garden that you want to develop, the plan will indicate both the shape of the bed and the planting positions (plant list supplied). The plants are then planted through the sheeting into the ground. The sheeting is covered with woodchips or pebbles on completion of planting. Customised templates can be ordered (see advertisement Pg 116) or you can choose from ready made designs.

Garden centres and nurseries

If you choose to do much of the work yourself visits to the Garden Centre will be very much a part of the DIY itinerary. Be careful to have an idea of what you require before you approach these centres. They always seem to be very busy at weekends, everyone wants to do their gardening on a Saturday. Your local plant supplier will have much more time to give you good advice if you call on a weekday! It is also wise to purchase plants early in the season when you will have a better selection available. An outline plan is always useful for your garden centre visit. A list of plants as supplied with planting templates is even more useful. A reliable garden centre in your area may be had by contacting your local garden centre association.

Landscaping is child's play

Problems and Solutions

Some ideas for dealing with problem sites.

Steep slopes

If there is enough topsoil on the slope you could consider naturalising the area with such plants as silver birch, rowan, alder, pine and beech or deciduous larch which would give very good autumn colour. These plants could be under planted with laurels, hollies or other such wide spreading shrubs that would keep weeds at bay. In time you could cut away some of the undergrowth to establish walkways or seating areas on the slope itself.

If there is very little soil on the slope itself, it may be screened off as in the diagram. This remedy can be very practical if the slope is unworkable.

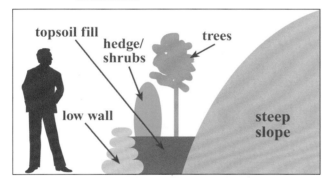

Wet areas

Do not despair if on first inspection your ground appears to be holding a lot of water. It is normal to find pools of water lodging after the builder has finished. This is normally due to compaction and ruts left after excavation have been carried out. Time will cure a lot of these problems and the cultivation and levelling of the ground during landscaping operations will remedy the vast majority of any remaining problems.

If you experience continuing problems with water logging then you should seek professional advice. It may be necessary to drain off surplus water, possibly using a pump. Alternatively, you will have to create a catchment area within your site which will act as an underground soakpit. An open catchment area can also be turned to advantage by incorporating it into a water feature.

There are lots of plants that will survive and even thrive in wet situations. When planting into wet conditions, it is normal to plant into soil heaps. These heaps can be created by hand or by mechanical digger during dry spells

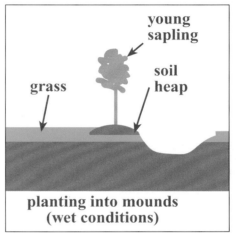

planting into mounds
(wet conditions)

Poor or very little topsoil

Generally this term refers to soil which is hard to work, has very little organic matter and is lacking in nutrients. Organic matter (farmyard manure, mosspeat, etc.) and nutrients are easily added to improve poor soil. Remember that grass will grow under most conditions, however, where you have very little depth or very poor topsoil you will need to fertilise on a more regular basis to keep your grass looking green.

Where you have very little topsoil, you should consider your options. Topsoiling the complete area can be prohibitively expensive. Gravel areas with planting pockets can be a good option when topsoil is scarce. Good colour can be achieved using planting pockets and spreading plants as in the photograph.

Exposed sites

When dealing with these sites, there are several options. Depending on the planning guidelines for the area, a man made shelter

Problems and Solutions

such as a wall or fence may be appropriate. The other alternative is to plant shelter bed trees.

It can be very expensive to build a fence or wall around your site just for shelter purposes and these are not always the most effective type of screening anyway. Another solution is to create a sheltered patio which will ensure that you can start enjoying your garden immediately. Longer term, you will have to look at establishing a shelter belt using plants.

Coastal Areas

The same principles apply for treating coastal exposure except you have to be selective in your choice of plants. Professional advice is essential for any coastal development

Boundary and shelter belt planting
Regardless of the size or exposure of your site, one of the first and most important decisions you will have to make is your choice of boundary plants. Here we recommend some plants and make some suggestions as to where they are best suited.

Escellonia   *Coastal*

Leylandii   *Good tall hedge*

Hedgerow style   *Good for wildlife*

Beech   *Rural*

Grisillinia   *Suburban*

Laurel   *Rural*

Berberis   *Suburban*

Mixed Shrubs   *Hedging alternative*

Pebble Mulch

Bark Mulch

Easy maintenance

Because of the busy lifestyles people lead today, great strides have been made in materials and gadgets to make gardening easier.

Mulches
Because of necessity, people are using mulches as an alternative weed control. These can be either used on their own or in conjunction with a mulch fabric.

Mowing edges
It often takes as long to trim the edges of a lawn as it does to cut the lawn itself. To cut down on the time involved in edges, it is important to get the right shape into the lawn. Create easy curves avoiding sharp corners where possible. A cutting strip installed at the early stages of the landscaping can be very beneficial. A narrow application of weedkiller around the edges of the lawn and particularly at base of walls and kerbs can be very effective although a little unsightly in a small garden. Modern strimmers are readily available and worth buying. The sharp lawn edge cut out with a spade or lawn edger is by far the most aesthetic. But, remember once you go this route, you will be trimming and cutting very regularly.

Plants for low maintenance
Some expert advice from a suitably qualified person is well worth your while at this stage. Here we look at different types of planting arrangements and grade them according to their ease of maintenance. Marked out of ten, a high mark in the illustration indicates easy maintenance.

Footpaths and walls

Should creepers be planted against the walls of houses? This is a question often asked. With modern building methods most walls will not be affected by creepers. The planting of creepers on walls is very much a matter of personal choice. Although they can be a bit troublesome with regards to maintenance, this is normally well outweighed by the character that they lend to a house.

Some creepers can spread rapidly so selection is very important. Gold Heart Ivy is a good choice for a self climber. Also consider using evergreen shrubs as climbers. They give the same effect and can easily be tied back when paintwork needs maintenance. It is wise to decide early about creepers as provision needs to be made for planting pockets. Good planting pockets will support dwarf shrubs at the base of climbers.

Footpaths are a consideration when establishing planting on the walls of a house. Traditional concrete paths do not lend themselves easily to planting pockets. Paving slabs are a good alternative to solid footpath. Awkward corners around a house are best planted rather than cutting paving to fit an area. Try planting the gap with dwarf plants or alpines.

Golden Heart Ivy

Evergreen shrubs, alternative for climbers

Dwarf shrubs for base of climbers

Awkward climbers

Alpine plants at base of wall

Change of levels

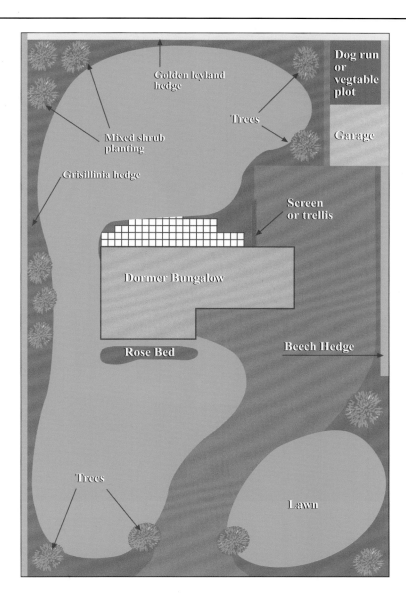

Landscaping Costs

Costing out a landscape project is difficult as sites vary so much. The final cost will depend on how elaborate your own tastes are. To eliminate the degree of error in this calculation we assume that initial site clearance and levelling/topsoiling has been carried out, and price includes only for completion of soft landscaping as outlined.

The outline plan opposite would need the following quantities of plants and mulch material.

- 11 ornamental trees
- 2 apple trees
- 50 Beech hedge
- 180 Grisillinia hedge
- 24 Golden leyland hedge
- 120 mixed shrubs
- 24 roses
- 15 heathers
- 3 Specimen conifers
- 3 Climbers for trellis
- 300 sq/mts weedsheet
- 15 cubic metres woodmulch

DIY cost for all above
£2,000.00

Landscape contractors cost
£4,000.00

Add approx. 50% extra for 1 acre.

Ordering landscape plans
Landscaping plans can be ordered through PLAN-A-HOME, in conjunction with house plan package orders.
(See enquiry sheet p159. For details.)

Summary:
- Budget for some landscaping, work can be completed in stages.
- A minimum budget to start work on a half acre site would start at around £2,000 using the services of a professional landscape contractor.
- The above costs are derived from consultation with experienced landscape contractors and are given as guidelines only.

All photgraphs and diagrams supplied by Walsh Landscapes, Derra, Kilkishen, Co. Clare. Telephone 061 367283.

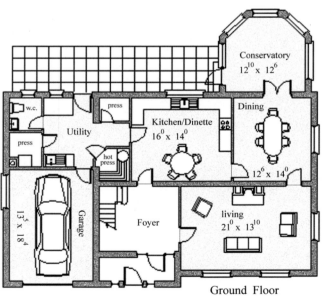

Ground Floor

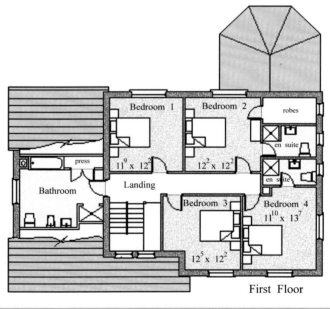

First Floor

Overall Length	50'07"
Overall Width	44'00"
Ground Floor	1322 sq.ft.
First Floor	1044 sq.ft.
Floor Area	2366 sq.ft.

This design is generously proportioned and has flexibility - the garage could be a children's play area or a second living space. The sun lounge at the rear would obviously require a sunny aspect to function as such.

Construction Costs
For a guideline of costs in Section C see pages 48 and 155.

Additional Options and Services Available. See page 17.

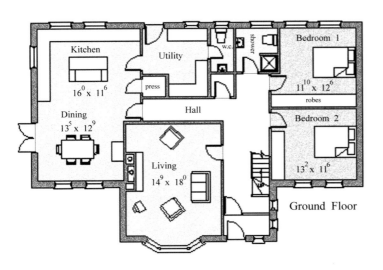

Kitchen
16^0 x 11^6

Utility

press

Dining
13^5 x 12^9

Hall

Living
14^9 x 18^0

w.c.

shower

Bedroom 1
11^{10} x 12^6
robes

Bedroom 2
13^2 x 11^6

Ground Floor

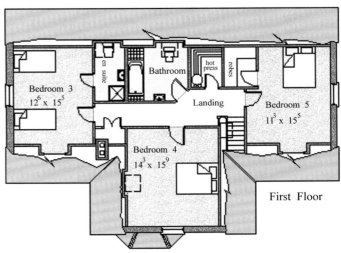

Bedroom 3
12^6 x 15^5

en suite

Bathroom

hot press

robes

Landing

Bedroom 4
14^3 x 15^9

Bedroom 5
11^3 x 15^5

First Floor

Construction Costs
For a guideline of costs in Section C see pages 48 and 155.

Much of the vernacular housing in Ireland have white rendered walls and pitched slate roofs. Planning guidelines for your area may make a recommendation on suitable external finishes.

Overall Length	51'06"
Overall Width	35'02"
Ground Floor	1412 sq.ft.
First Floor	955 sq.ft.
Floor Area	2367 sq.ft.

Additional Options and Services Available. See page 17.

133

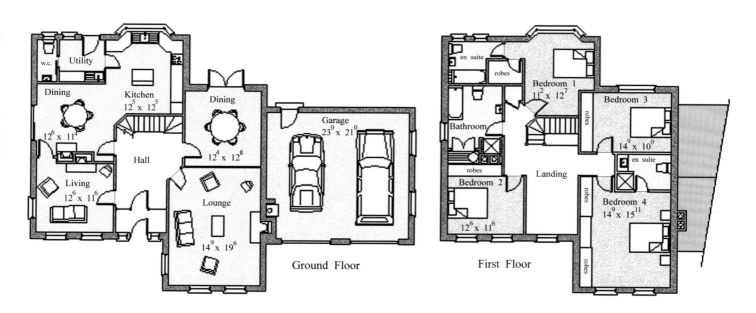

Ground Floor

First Floor

Overall Length	62'02"
Overall Width	43'00"
Ground Floor	1205 sq.ft.
First Floor	1169 sq.ft.
Floor Area	2374 sq.ft.

A separate dining room is a requirement for many people. Page 13 has some information on planning this type of room.

Construction Costs
For a guideline of costs in Section C see pages 48 and 155.

Additional Options and Services Available. See page 17.

Five Bedroom

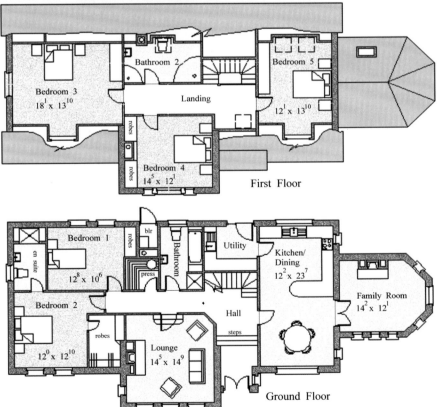

First Floor

- Bedroom 3 18^1 x 13^{10}
- Bathroom 2
- Landing
- Bedroom 5 12^1 x 13^{10}
- Bedroom 4 14^5 x 12^1

Ground Floor

- Bedroom 1 12^8 x 10^6
- en suite
- robes
- blr
- press
- Bathroom
- Utility
- Kitchen/Dining 12^2 x 23^7
- Family Room 14^2 x 12^1
- Bedroom 2 12^0 x 12^{10}
- robes
- Hall
- steps
- Lounge 14^5 x 14^9

Plan-A-Home
For Construction Cost
Consultants and
Quantity Surveyors.

Arched window and door openings and a stone
finished annex are distinguishing features of this
design.

Overall Length	69'08"
Overall Width	31'00"
Ground Floor	1517 sq.ft.
First Floor	858 sq.ft.
Floor Area	2375 sq.ft.

Additional Options and Services Available. See page 17.

Ground Floor

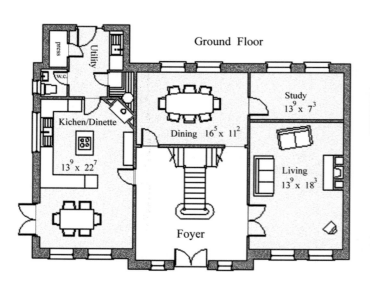

press

Utility

w.c.

Kichen/Dinette

13⁹ x 22⁷

Dining 16⁵ x 11²

Study
13⁹ x 7³

Living
13⁹ x 18³

Foyer

First Floor

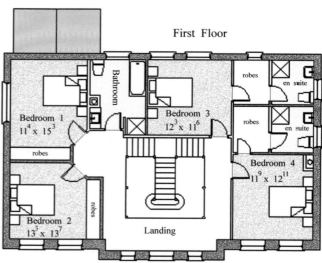

Bathroom

robes

en suite

Bedroom 1
11⁴ x 15³

Bedroom 3
12³ x 11⁶

robes

en suite

robes

Bedroom 4
11⁹ x 12¹¹

robes

Bedroom 2
13³ x 13⁷

Landing

Overall Length	46'07"
Overall Width	35'02"
Ground Floor	1297 sq.ft.
First Floor	1105 sq.ft.
Floor Area	2402 sq.ft.

A dramatic central staircase a surrounding balcony distinguish the large hallway of this house. Heating may be an important consideration with an open space of this size.

Plan-A-Home
For Complete Site
Survey and Analysis.

Additional Options and Services Available. See page 17.

136

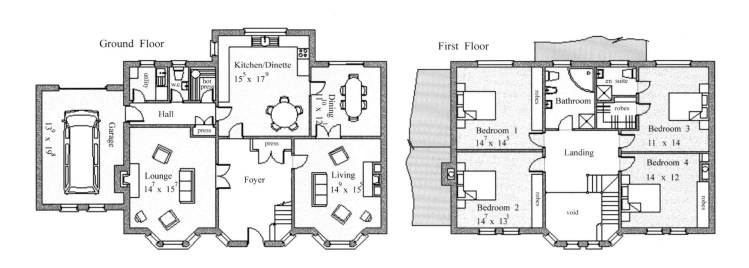

Ground Floor

utility

w.c.

hot press

Kitchen/Dinette
15⁵ x 17⁹

Hall

press

Dining
11¹⁰ x 12¹

Garage
13⁹ x 19⁸

Lounge
14⁷ x 15⁷

press

Foyer

Living
14⁹ x 15

First Floor

robes

Bathroom

en suite

robes

Bedroom 1
14⁷ x 14⁵

Landing

Bedroom 3
11 x 14

Bedroom 4
14 x 12

Bedroom 2
14⁷ x 13¹

robes

void

robes

Construction Costs
For a guideline of costs
in Section C see pages
48 and 155.

Large bathrooms are increasingly required to
facilitate whirlpool baths, steam showers and
other luxury fittings. See our Luxury Bathroom
editorial on page 72 for ideas.

Overall Length 58'03''
Overall Width 37'09''
Ground Floor 1326 sq.ft.
First Floor 1103 sq.ft.
Floor Area 2429 sq.ft.

Additional Options and Services Available. See page 17.

137

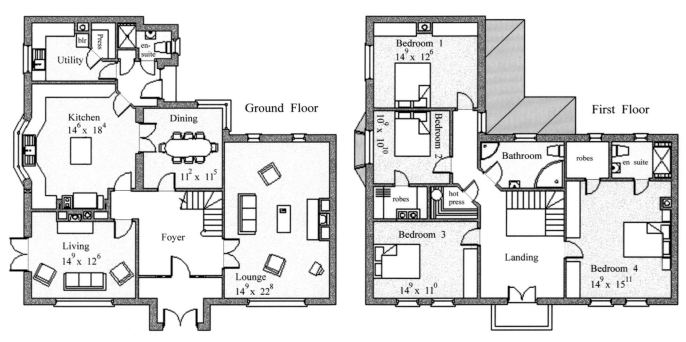

Ground Floor

Utility

Kitchen
14⁶ x 18⁴

Dining
11² x 11⁵

Living
14⁹ x 12⁶

Foyer

Lounge
14⁹ x 22⁸

First Floor

Bedroom 1
14⁹ x 12⁶

Bedroom 2
10⁹ x 10¹⁰

Bathroom

robes

en suite

Bedroom 3
14⁹ x 11⁰

Landing

Bedroom 4
14⁹ x 15¹¹

Overall Length	44'00"
Overall Width	42'00"
Ground Floor	1335 sq.ft.
First Floor	1155 sq.ft.
Floor Area	2510 sq.ft.

A low parapet wall allows the creation of a step out balcony above the entrance porch of this house. Planning regulations may govern whether or not this is appropriate to your site.

Construction Costs
For a guideline of costs in Section C see pages 48 and 155.

Additional Options and Services Available. See page 17.

Four Bedroom

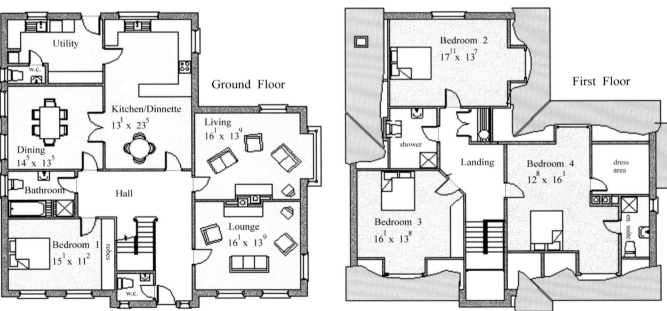

Ground Floor

Utility

w.c.

Kitchen/Dinnette
13^1 x 23^5

Living
16^1 x 13^9

Dining
14^5 x 13^5

Bathroom

Hall

robes

Bedroom 1
15^1 x 11^2

Lounge
16^1 x 13^9

w.c.

First Floor

Bedroom 2
17^{11} x 13^7

shower

Landing

Bedroom 4
12^8 x 16^1

dress area

Bedroom 3
16^1 x 13^8

en suite

Plan-A-Home
For Interior Planning
and Design.

Connections and views between rooms are important.
You may wish to consider using glazed panels instead
of solid walls. Open plan spaces can be defined
simply by a change in the floor surface.

Overall Length 46'03"
Overall Width 44'06"
Ground Floor 1678 sq.ft.
First Floor 1135 sq.ft.
Floor Area 2813 sq.ft.

Additional Options and Services Available. See page 17.

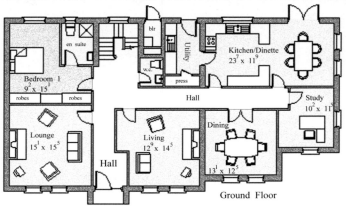

Ground Floor

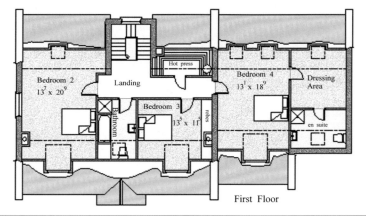

First Floor

Overall Length	61'04"
Overall Width	32'09"
Ground Floor	1727 sq.ft.
First Floor	1200 sq.ft.
Floor Area	2927 sq.ft.

This dormer dwelling is fundamentally traditional in its appearance. Internally the layout offers plenty of scope to adapt spaces to your requirements.

Plan-A-Home
For Construction
Supervision.

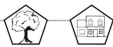

Additional Options and Services Available. See page 17.

140

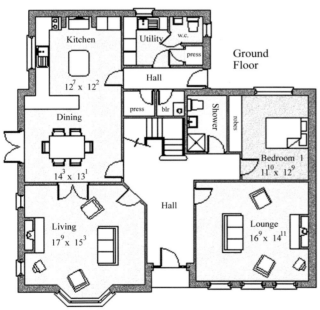

Kitchen 12⁷ x 12²

Utility w.c. press

Ground Floor

Hall

press blr

Shower robes

Dining 14³ x 13¹

Bedroom 1 11¹⁰ x 12⁹

Living 17⁹ x 15³

Hall

Lounge 16⁹ x 14¹¹

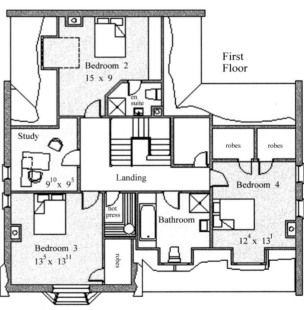

Bedroom 2 15 x 9

First Floor

en suite

Study 9¹⁰ x 9⁵

Landing

robes robes

Bedroom 4 12⁴ x 13¹

hot press

Bathroom

Bedroom 3 13⁵ x 13¹¹

robes

Construction Costs
For a guideline of costs in Section C see pages 48 and 155.

It is important to preserve the natural elements of a site. Existing indigenous plants can be trimmed and tamed to form part of a new planting scheme.

Overall Length 44'00"
Overall Width 42'11"
Ground Floor 1482 sq.ft.
First Floor 1163 sq.ft.
Floor Area 2645 sq.ft.

Additional Options and Services Available. See page 17.

141

Five Bedroom

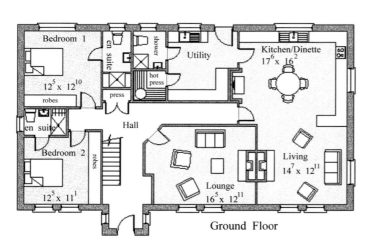

Bedroom 1

en suite

shower

Utility

Kitchen/Dinette
17^6 x 16^2

12^5 x 12^{10}

robes

hot press

press

en suite

Hall

Bedroom 2

robes

Living
14^7 x 12^{11}

12^5 x 11^1

Lounge
16^5 x 12^{11}

Ground Floor

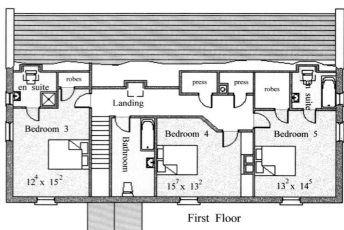

en suite

robes

press   press   robes   en suite

Landing

Bedroom 3

Bathroom

Bedroom 4

Bedroom 5

12^4 x 15^2

15^7 x 13^2

13^2 x 14^5

First Floor

Overall Length	54'05"
Overall Width	31'02"
Ground Floor	1555 sq.ft.
First Floor	1017 sq.ft.
Floor Area	2572 sq.ft.

The farmhouse kitchen which serves as kitchen, dining and living space is growing in popularity. See page 13 on planning a multi-functional kitchen.

Construction Costs
For a guideline of costs in Section C see pages 48 and 155.

Additional Options and Services Available. See page 17.

Four Bedroom

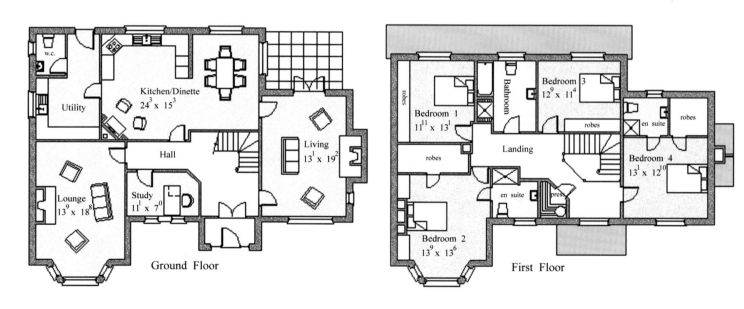

Ground Floor

- w.c.
- Utility
- Kitchen/Dinette 24³ x 15³
- Hall
- Living 13¹ x 19²
- Lounge 13⁹ x 18⁸
- Study 11¹ x 7⁰

First Floor

- robes
- Bedroom 1 11¹¹ x 13¹
- Bathroom
- Bedroom 3 12⁹ x 11⁴
- robes
- en suite
- robes
- Landing
- Bedroom 4 13¹ x 12¹⁰
- robes
- en suite
- press
- Bedroom 2 13⁹ x 13⁶

Plan-A-Home
For Comprehensive
Specification
Documents.

Many of our layouts allocate space for a range, aga or
stove. See page 68 for further details.

Overall Length	50'01"
Overall Width	37'11"
Ground Floor	1414 sq.ft.
First Floor	1180 sq.ft.
Floor Area	2594 sq.ft.

Additional Options and Services Available. See page 17.

Five Bedroom

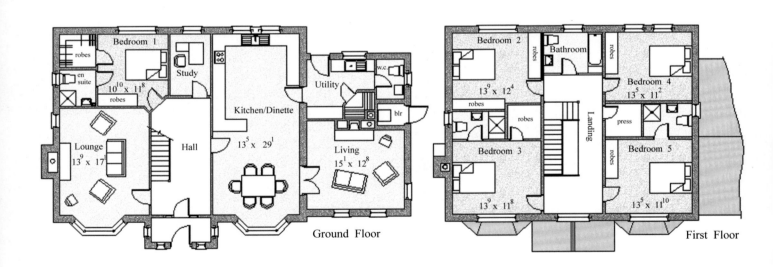

Ground Floor

First Floor

Overall Length	55'02"
Overall Width	35'02"
Ground Floor	1525 sq.ft.
First Floor	1076 sq.ft.
Floor Area	2601 sq.ft.

A single storey wing facilitates a living room, utility, hot press and cloakroom to this two storey dwelling.

<u>Plan-A-Home</u>
Have offices in Dublin, Cork, Galway and Co. Donegal. See inside back cover for details.

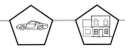

Additional Options and Services Available. See page 17.

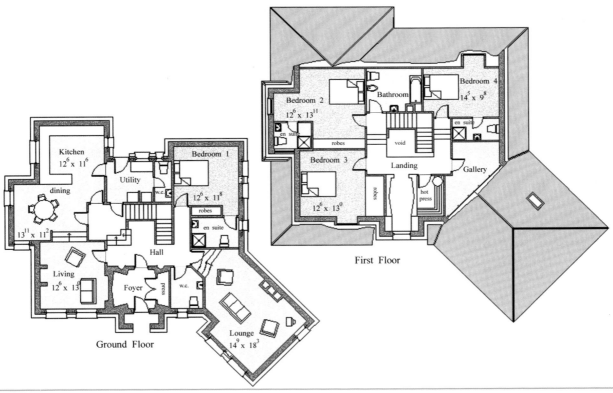

Ground Floor

Kitchen
12⁶ x 11⁶

Utility

dining

13¹¹ x 11²

Living
12⁶ x 13

Foyer

w.c.

press

Hall

w.c.

Bedroom 1

12⁶ x 11⁸

robes

en suite

Lounge
14⁹ x 18³

First Floor

Bedroom 2
12⁶ x 13¹¹

en suite

Bathroom

Bedroom 4
14⁵ x 9⁸

en suite

robes

void

Bedroom 3
12⁶ x 13⁰

robes

Landing

hot press

Gallery

<u>Construction Costs</u>
For a guideline of costs in Section C see pages 48 and 155.

Unusual internal spaces are a feature of this design. The entrance walls are curved, natural light enters through rooflights and a balcony enters onto the living room.

Overall Length	41'04"
Overall Width	39'05"
Ground Floor	1500 sq.ft.
First Floor	1068 sq.ft.
Floor Area	2568 sq.ft.

For a metric/imperial conversion table see page 17.

Five Bedroom

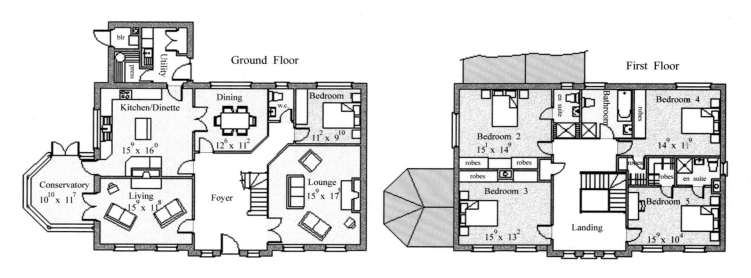

Ground Floor

blr

press

Utility

Kitchen/Dinette
15⁹ x 16⁰

Dining
12⁶ x 11²

w.c.

Bedroom
11² x 9¹⁰

Conservatory
10¹⁰ x 11⁷

Living
15⁹ x 11⁸

Foyer

Lounge
15⁹ x 17

First Floor

Bedroom 2
15¹ x 14⁹

en suite

Bathroom

robes

Bedroom 4
14⁹ x 11⁹

robes   robes

robes

robes

Bedroom 3

en suite

Bedroom 5
15⁹ x 10⁴

15⁹ x 13²

Landing

Overall Length	47'09"
Overall Width	40'04"
Ground Floor	1480 sq.ft.
First Floor	1177 sq.ft.
Floor Area	2657 sq.ft.

Most plan layouts can be altered to facilitate an integral garage. Here a garage could be built on and accessed through the utility room.

Construction Costs
For a guideline of costs in Section C see pages 48 and 155.

Additional Options and Services Available. See page 17.

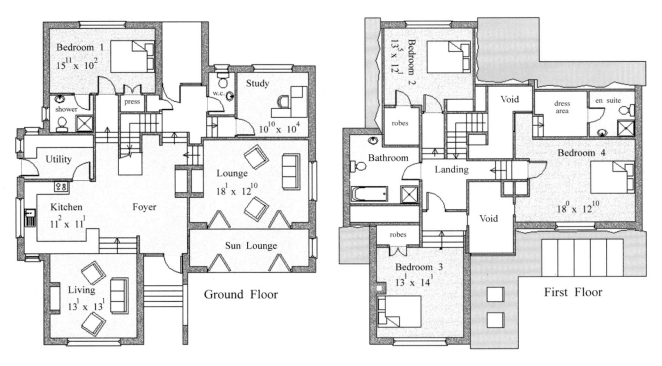

Ground Floor

Bedroom 1
15^{11} x 10^2

shower

press

w.c.

Study
10^{10} x 10^4

Utility

Lounge
18^1 x 12^{10}

Kitchen
11^2 x 11^1

Foyer

Sun Lounge

Living
13^1 x 13^1

First Floor

Bedroom 2
13^5 x 12^1

Void

dress area

en suite

robes

Bathroom

Landing

Bedroom 4
18^0 x 12^{10}

Void

robes

Bedroom 3
13^1 x 14^1

<u>Plan-A-Home</u>
For Landscape Design.

The sun lounge to this multi-level, contemporary house is formed off the lounge. Folding glazed doors allow the space to open up on to the garden in the summer months.

Overall Length 44'11"
Overall Width 50'02"
Ground Floor 1479 sq.ft.
First Floor 1177 sq.ft.
Floor Area 2656 sq.ft.

Additional Options and Services Available. See page 17.

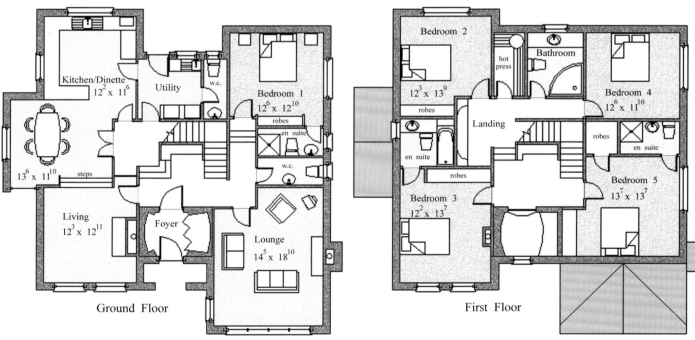

Ground Floor

Kitchen/Dinette
12^2 x 11^6

Utility

w.c.

Bedroom 1
12^6 x 12^{10}

robes

en suite

w.c.

13^6 x 11^{10}

steps

Living
12^3 x 12^{11}

Foyer

Lounge
14^5 x 18^{10}

First Floor

Bedroom 2
12^3 x 13^9

robes

hot press

Bathroom

Bedroom 4
12^6 x 11^{10}

Landing

robes

en suite

en suite

robes

Bedroom 3
12^2 x 13^7

Bedroom 5
13^7 x 13^7

Overall Length	44'00"
Overall Width	44'06"
Ground Floor	1356 sq.ft.
First Floor	1210 sq.ft.
Floor Area	2566 sq.ft.

A large window in the living room gable allows
a glimpse of the exposed timber trusses in the
room beyond.

<u>Plan-A-Home</u>
For exciting new
designs.

Ground Floor

Living
13⁷ x 15⁴

Kitchen/Dinette
14⁹ x 10³

10⁶ x 15⁴

hot press | blr

Utility

Foyer

press

shower

Study
9¹⁰ x 9⁸

Lounge
16⁵ x 14⁹

robes

Bedroom 1
11⁰ x 16⁵

en suite

en suite

Bedroom 2
13⁷ x 12⁶

robes

Bedroom 3
10⁸ x 16⁵

robes

Landing

Bath

Bedroom 4
10¹⁰ x 19⁰

en-suite

First Floor

<u>Construction Costs</u>
For a guideline of costs
in Section C see pages
48 and 155.

A contemporary design with a traditional flavour.
This layout is intended to take advantage of the sun
throughout the day.

Overall Length 50'07"
Overall Width   52'10"
Ground Floor   1396 sq.ft.
First Floor   1124 sq.ft.
Floor Area   2520 sq.ft.

Additional Options and Services Available. See page 17.

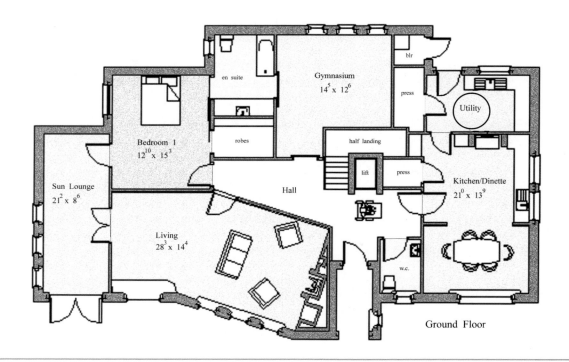

Ground Floor

Overall Length	65'04"
Overall Width	41'11"
Ground Floor	1947 sq.ft.
First Floor	1540 sq.ft.
Floor Area	3487 sq.ft.

This house has been designed specifically to suit the needs of a client who is a wheelchair user. We have chosen to include it in this publication in order to illustrate how the particular requirements of an individual can be met. The basic requirement here is ease of circulation. Doorways are wider than those shown on standard plans and sliding doors which are easier to negotiate have been specified.

Internal view from sun lounge

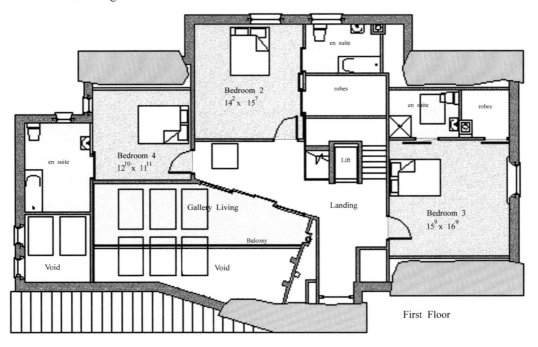

First Floor

The master bedroom has en-suite facilities with access through to the gymnasium. A lift and stairs have been provided. It is important that the needs of all users are met. As the client spends a large amount of time at home, it is paramount to create pleasant and functional spaces such as the study area in the living room, the sun lounge and gallery. Finally automated roof lights open up to give a feeling of airiness to the gallery space.

<u>Construction Costs</u>
For a guideline of costs in Section C see pages 48 and 155.

Additional Options and Services Available. See page 17.

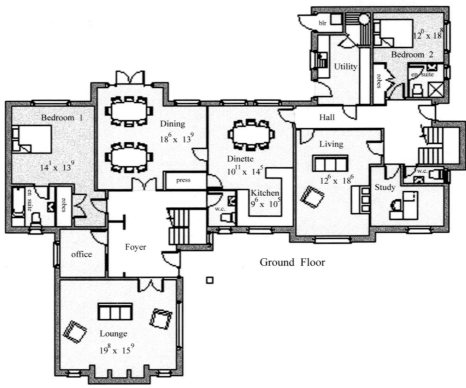

Ground Floor

Rooms labelled on plan:
- Bedroom 1 — 14¹ x 13⁹
- Dining — 18⁶ x 13⁹
- Dinette — 10¹¹ x 14⁵
- Kitchen — 9⁶ x 10⁵
- Living — 12⁶ x 18⁶
- Study
- Bedroom 2 — 12⁰ x 18⁸
- Utility
- Hall
- Foyer
- office
- Lounge — 19⁸ x 15⁹
- press
- w.c.
- en suite
- robes
- blr

Overall Length	75'02"
Overall Width	64'08"
Ground Floor	2494 sq.ft.
First Floor	2494 sq.ft.
Floor Area	4988 sq.ft.

Plan-A-Home have substantial experience in the field of guest house accommodation. There is an increasing demand for large dwellings comprising six bedrooms and upwards. As guest houses tend to be of a greater capacity than standard dwellings; a site which is suitable in terms of size and servicing is paramount. Internally room sizes and facilities

Additional Options and Services Available. See page 17.

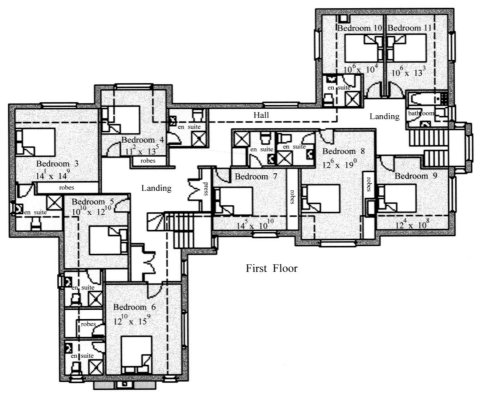

Bedroom 10
10^6 x 10^4

Bedroom 11
10^6 x 13^3

en suite

bathroom

Hall

Landing

en suite

Bedroom 4
11^2 x 13^5

robes

en suite   en suite

Bedroom 3
14^1 x 14^9

robes

Bedroom 8
12^6 x 19^0

robes

Landing

press

en suite

Bedroom 5
10^{10} x 12^{10}

Bedroom 7

robes

Bedroom 9
12^4 x 10^8

en suite

14^5 x 10^{10}

First Floor

en suite

Bedroom 6
12^{10} x 15^9

robes

en suite

must meet with Bord Failte requirements. It may be desirable to have family accommodation separate to, but accessible from the guest accommodation. A Planning Application of this type differs from 'standard applications'. Our staff will be able to give guidance on all of these issues. Information on Registration, fees and regulations governing guest houses is available from Bord Failte Eireann, Dublin.

<u>Construction Costs</u>
For a guideline of costs in Section C see pages 48 and 155.

Five Bedroom

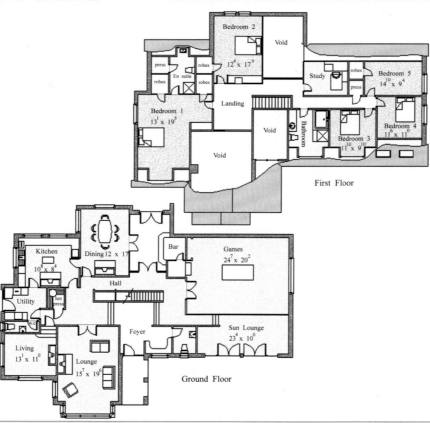

First Floor

Ground Floor

Overall Length	74'06''
Overall Width	56'00''
Ground Floor	2638 sq.ft.
First Floor	1638 sq.ft.
Floor Area	4276 sq.ft.

This contemporary design incorporates a large games room, luxury bathroom and sun lounge. Views are afforded into the living and bar rooms from the landing above.

<u>Construction Costs</u>
For a guideline of costs in Section C see pages 48 and 155.

Additional Options and Services Available. See page 17.

Guideline Specifications
Section C

Stage A

Roof: Tegral 2000 Slates.
External Walls: smooth render.
Fascia/soffit: upvc or aluminium.
Windows/external doors: upvc double glazed.
Internal doors: Hardwood panel.
Architrave/skirting: Hardwood.

Stage B

All as detailed on page 48 including for:
Hardwood kitchen/utility units;
2400mm high wall tiling to baths, showers &
W.C.'s including 500mm tiling above
worktops.
Decoration to all external/internal walls,
ceilings and second fix joinery only.

Stage C

Siteworks as detailed with gravel drive & kerbs.

plan	stage	region 1	region 2	region 3
5061	A	127,041	142,286	157,937
	B	156,401	175,169	194,437
	C	168,957	189,232	210,048
5062	A	120,036	134,441	149,229
	B	151,456	169,630	188,290
	C	166,824	186,843	207,396
5063	A	137,251	153,722	170,631
	B	166,608	186,601	207,127
	C	180,441	202,093	224,324
5064	A	155,651	174,330	193,506
	B	176,160	197,299	219,002
	C	185,802	208,099	230,990
5065	A	132,953	148,907	165,287
	B	160,977	180,294	200,127
	C	176,471	197,647	219,388
5066	A	151,047	169,173	187,782
	B	180,929	202,641	224,931
	C	196,298	219,854	244,038
5067	A	133,894	149,961	166,457
	B	164,716	184,482	204,775
	C	180,085	201,695	223,882
5068	A	141,175	158,116	175,509
	B	169,936	190,329	211,265
	C	184,187	206,290	228,982
5069	A	150,746	168,836	187,407
	B	184,148	206,246	228,933
	C	198,670	222,510	246,986
5070	A	135,047	151,252	167,890
	B	164,808	184,585	204,890
	C	178,638	200,075	222,083
5071	A	120,962	135,477	150,380
	B	158,919	177,989	197,568
	C	172,413	193,103	214,344
5072	A	132,675	148,596	164,942
	B	163,508	183,129	203,273
	C	176,293	197,448	219,167

Please Note: The prices listed here are for guideline purposes only and are indicative of contract values in €uro's current at Spring 2003.

plan	stage	region 1	region 2	region 3
5073	A	127,837	143,177	158,927
	B	165,499	185,359	205,748
	C	179,019	200,501	222,556
5074	A	160,568	176,625	194,288
	B	201,334	221,467	243,614
	C	217,820	239,602	263,562
5075	A	155,252	173,882	193,009
	B	188,086	210,657	233,829
	C	203,455	227,870	252,935
5076	A	142,569	159,678	177,242
	B	179,336	200,856	222,951
	C	194,705	218,069	242,057
5077	A	136,845	153,266	170,125
	B	175,051	196,057	217,623
	C	190,420	213,270	236,730
5078	A	135,573	151,842	168,545
	B	172,123	192,778	213,984
	C	187,491	209,990	233,089
5079	A	173,085	193,885	215,179
	B	214,221	239,928	266,320
	C	235,738	264,026	293,069
5080	A	258,340	289,341	321,169
	B	324,226	363,134	403,078
	C	347,524	289,227	432,042
5081	A	246,333	275,893	306,241
	B	288,913	323,583	359,177
	C	308,646	345,684	383,709

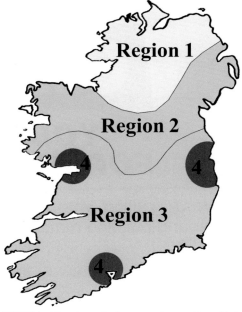

NOTE: Region 4 (areas in red) - It is currently impossible to accurately predict pricing trends in these areas. However, developments in region 4 may increase by up to 10% to 20 % of region 3.
Other cities may also experience similar trends of escalating construction costs.

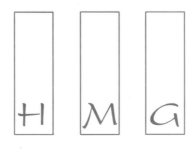

QS Division

Office 8b The Courtyard
Lower Main Street
Letterkenny
Co. Donegal
email: lkenny@hmg.ie
tel: 074 9127844
fax: 074 9127841

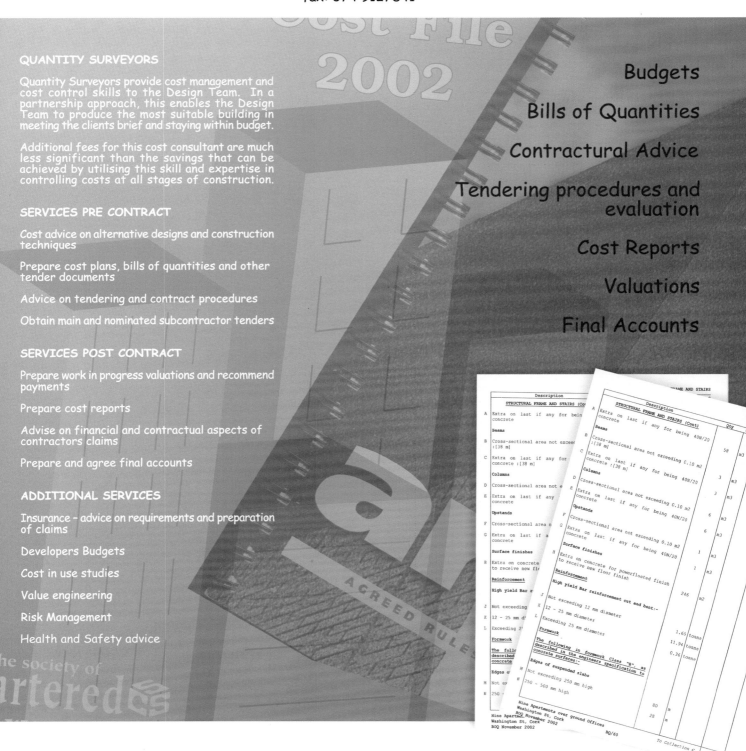

QUANTITY SURVEYORS

Quantity Surveyors provide cost management and cost control skills to the Design Team. In a partnership approach, this enables the Design Team to produce the most suitable building in meeting the clients brief and staying within budget.

Additional fees for this cost consultant are much less significant than the savings that can be achieved by utilising this skill and expertise in controlling costs at all stages of construction.

SERVICES PRE CONTRACT

Cost advice on alternative designs and construction techniques

Prepare cost plans, bills of quantities and other tender documents

Advice on tendering and contract procedures

Obtain main and nominated subcontractor tenders

SERVICES POST CONTRACT

Prepare work in progress valuations and recommend payments

Prepare cost reports

Advise on financial and contractual aspects of contractors claims

Prepare and agree final accounts

ADDITIONAL SERVICES

Insurance – advice on requirements and preparation of claims

Developers Budgets

Cost in use studies

Value engineering

Risk Management

Health and Safety advice

Budgets

Bills of Quantities

Contractural Advice

Tendering procedures and evaluation

Cost Reports

Valuations

Final Accounts

Quantity Surveyors   Construction Economists

PLANNING PERMISSION
(Republic of Ireland)

After choosing your site, and having given some thought as to the nature of the development, the first stage is to apply for planning permission to the Planning Authority in your county, or to the Urban District Council, or in the case of cities, to the City Borough Corporation.

There are three types of planning application which can be made, i.e. outline, approval and full permission, and these are outlined below.

OUTLINE PERMISSION

In some cases, persons may wish to ascertain whether or not planning permission would be granted for a particular development/site. On the advice of your architect/ engineer, it may be prudent to apply for outline permission to determine whether or not your development would be permitted. Outline permission allows you to make an application without going to the expense of preparing house plans.

An outline permission must be accompanied by:-
a) A complete application form.
b) A relevant fee.
c) Proposed site layout and location maps, showing location of proposed development on site, and giving brief description of same.
d) 2 copies of notice of application to Planning Authority inserted in local newspaper and 2 no. copies site notice.
Note:- Grant of outline permission does not permit carrying out of any works.

APPROVAL

Approval can only be sought where outline permission as described above, has already been granted, and must be accompanied by complete working drawings and specification, together with all documents as listed for outline permission.

FULL PERMISSION

Full permission is a combination of outline and approval as previously described and is a more direct and speedier method for sites where it is considered that planning permission should be relatively easy to obtain.
Details of complete documents required for planning applications, as follows:-
a) Complete application form, completed accurately, stating all details as requested.
b) Completed application Fee form, with remittance
c) 4 no. copies of plans, elevations, site maps, site location maps and 2 no. copies of newspaper notice, site notice and letter from Group Scheme if applicable.
d) Local Needs Form (applicable to some Counties)
e) A Soil Suitability/Permeability Test. Applicable to some sites.
Any other information considered relevent to your Application.

GENERAL PROCEDURE

Should the Planning Authority decide that insufficient information has been supplied they are entitled to request further information. Your application is then put on hold until the relevent information has been received, this should be supplied within four weeks. The council are then obliged to give their decision within eight weeks of this. Planning approval is then issued one month later.

PUBLIC NOTICE

This is done by means of notification in a locally distributed newspaper and also with a notice on site, placed in a convenient position so as to be ledgible from main thoroughfare, and must remain in place for a period of one month of the application. 2 no. copies of each to be submitted with application for planning.

SITE LAYOUT MAPS

4 layout maps, clearly showing boundaries of the site, site entrance, storm and foul drainage details, water supply etc. A Letter of consent from any group schemes or landowners to right-of-ways must accompany the application. Proven site lines are also required to be shown on the map.

SITE LOCATION MAPS

4 no. site location maps, being extracts from Ordnance Survey sheets, and showing clearly the location of site and adjoining developments in relation to any churches, crossroads, towns or any other distinct landmark in the area. Outline of site to be marked in red and overall landowners holding outlined in blue.

HOUSE PLANS

4 no. copies of detailed plans and specifications, clearly illustrating layout, elevations, sections, details of finishes, and all materials to be used in the construction.

OBJECTION

Objection can be made in writing as follows:-
a) By the applicant to the Planning Authority in relation to it's decision to refuse, or to object to some of the conditions relevant to the Grant of Permission. The applicant has one month from the date of receipt of a decision, within which to object.
b) Objections can be lodged by a third party against a planning application, and if an objection is made, the objector is notified of the Councils decision, at which stage he has a further 21 days to appeal the Council's decision.

This information is a simple guide. It is advisable to contact your local Planning Office who will be glad to assist you with full relevant information concerning your application. Most Local Authorities have adopted Development Plans for their Counties.
These documents should ascertain whether or not a Planning Application relating to your circumstances should succeed.

ORDER FORM

OR ORDER ON LINE WWW.PLAN-A-HOME.IE

This form is to be used for direct ordering of unaltered plans.
(If you require plans to be altered please see page 5)

FOR PLAN COSTS CALL 1890 222345 or 1850 222345
(00 353 74 9129651 outside Eire)

Design No.

Planning Drawings (6 sets of plans)	€
Working Drawings (4 sets of plans & 4 sets of specification)	€
Reverse hand layout €100.00 extra.	€
Bill of quantities (Optional)	€
Total	€
Vat @ 21%	€
Total Due	€

Payment Details:

Cheque ☐ Postal Order ☐   Account No: _____

Credit Card ☐ Type [____]   Expiry Date: _____

Cardholders Signature: _____

Name: _____   **Site Address:** _____

Address: _____   _____

_____   _____

_____

Tel. No: _____   **e-mail:** _____

Please post to:

PLAN-A-HOME
Lower Main Street,
Letterkenny,
Co. Donegal.
Ireland.

Other Items required for planning permission:

6 sets of site layout/location map.
2 copies of site notice.
2 copies of newspaper notice.
Fully completed application form.
Planning application fee.
Percolation test (dependent on Local Authority)

Should you require any assistance with the above requirements contact any of the appointed Architectural offices listed inside the back cover.

Please complete your Specification list over leaf.

SPECIFICATION

Please tick the following to enable us to complete a detailed specification to suit your requirements (otherwise we will allow for a standard, good quality finish throughout).

Roof Covering:

tiles	- concrete	☐	slates	- synthetic	☐
	- clay	☐		- natural	☐ other _____

Windows:

hardwood	☐	uPVC	☐	aluminium	☐ other _____

External Doors\Frames:

hardwood	☐	uPVC	☐	aluminium	☐ other _____

External Finish:

dry dash	☐	smooth render	☐	brick (only if illustrated)	☐
wet dash	☐			stone (only if illustrated)	☐

Fascia, Soffit, Barge:

softwood	☐	aluminium	☐	
hardwood	☐	uPVC	☐ other _____	

Second-fix-Joinery:

sapelle doors	☐	hardwood panel doors	☐	
raised panel doors (regency)	☐		other _____	

Second-Fix-joinery Timbers:

softwood	☐	MDF	☐	
hardwood	☐		other _____	

Garage Doors:

hardwood	☐	roller shutter	☐	
overhead & insulated	☐	remote control	☐ other _____	

Heating:

oil	☐	electric	☐	
gas	☐	solid fuel	☐ underfloor	☐